CARIBBEAN
WINTER

CARIBBEAN WINTER

PAUL MORAND

Translation & Introduction by Mary Gallagher

Signal

Signal Books
Oxford

First published in French by
Ernest Flammarion as *Hiver caraïbe*, 1929

This English language edition first published in the United Kingdom
in 2018 by

Signal Books Limited
36 Minster Road
Oxford OX4 1LY
www.signalbooks.co.uk

© Flammarion, Paris, 1929
© Translation and Introduction: Mary Gallagher, 2018

A catalogue record for this book is available from the British Library.

The publication of this book was generously supported by an award
from the National University of Ireland.

ISBN 978-1-909930-68-1 Paper

Cover Design: Tora Kelly
Typesetting: Tora Kelly
Cover Image: © French Lines Collection
Printed in India by Imprint Digital Ltd

CONTENTS

INTRODUCTION

Who was Paul Morand?

The profile of the French writer Paul Morand (1888-1976) is complicated. He is known first and foremost as the prolific author of elegant, cosmopolitan stories and novels, and of stylish and worldly essays on subjects as diverse as Venice, Coco Chanel and New York. However, he is also infamous as a politically controversial figure, whose willing diplomatic collaboration with Vichy France, probably more than his unexceptional failure to distance himself from the ambient anti-Semitism of 1920s and 1930s France, led to his post-war fall from grace. Like its indefatigable author (of about one hundred books), Morand's writing is difficult to pigeonhole. In terms of genre, it spanned both fiction and non-fiction. Yet, while Morand launched his literary career with poetry, a genre quickly abandoned for short prose fiction, and while the latter brought him early and long-lived renown, it is true that, throughout his life, he wrote slightly more non-fiction than fiction. He was, above all, a keen-eyed traveller and his peregrinations, which were wide-ranging, covering not just Europe, Asia and Africa, but also North, Central and South America, including the Caribbean basin, were perhaps the main source of inspiration for his writing. Most of his essays, especially the travelogues, are presented in the same copiously cross-referenced, often acerbic, sometimes inscrutable dressing, always quick-fired and vivid and frequently ironic.

In our times of political correctness and 'trigger warnings', it is important to stress that *Hiver caraïbe* (*Caribbean Winter*) presents a pervasive racism. First of all, racial difference is perhaps the dominant concern of the book as a whole. Morand focuses in particular on the distinction between Blacks and Whites and, most crucially, on its preservation from the attrition or dilution of miscegenation. Secondly, he manages to include in his narrative a number of apparently gratuitous remarks about individuals whom he identifies as Jews. In this work, certainly, Morand confines himself to what might be called the 'fashionable anti-Semitism of the 1920s'[1] and his racist perspective on African America is entirely overt and unashamed but not, on the whole, pejorative. It is important to recognize that, in *Hiver caraïbe*, the anti-Semitism is limited to labelling people as Jews. Although the descriptions that he offers of these people are not, per se, derogatory, the dangers inherent in such routine labelling and indeed its cataclysmic historical consequences, need scarcely be underlined. Furthermore, it has to be said that other writings by Morand, more especially his posthumous journals and correspondence, clearly cross the charitable boundary that has been drawn between writers 'whose work reflected negative Jewish stereotypes'[2] and authors whose racism was more 'virulent' and toxic, many of whom were Morand's friends. In addition, *Hiver caraïbe* is not exempt from racist vitriol. This is reserved, however, for those whom Morand reviles, or at least pities and deplores, as being of 'mixed race'. Ironically, in *Hiver caraïbe*, he explicitly identifies these harbingers of his nightmare scenario, namely the 'filthy [sic] epoch of the half-caste'[3], not as 'coloured', but very emphatically as 'grey'. A full appraisal of the author's racism and its context lies beyond the scope of this Introduction. However, it is worth wondering if the almost facetious irresponsibility of Morand's

---

1   Milton Hindus, 'F. Scott Fitzgerald and Literary anti-Semitism' in *Commentary*, June 1947, pp. 508-16.

2   William Brustein, *Roots of Hate: Anti-Semitism in Europe before the Holocaust*, Cambridge: Cambridge University Press, 2003, p. 125.

3   In *Rien que la terre*, Paris: Grasset, 1926. See below p.74 for Morand's elaboration in *Hiver caraïbe* on this incendiary comment.

particular brand of 'fashionable' racism – and, indeed, a certain posterity's irresponsibility in wishing to overlook it – might be best accounted for by what one singularly astute commentator has identified as the explanation of 1930s French literary anti-Semitism in general: namely, the fact that the imperative of 'French literature since Baudelaire has been to relieve tedium (rather than to promote justice)'[4].

Hiver caraïbe was published in 1929, towards the end of what was without question the most intense period of Morand's travel-writing life. The two journeys that inspired the Caribbean travel journal, trips to the Caribbean and its continental hinterland, took place in very early and very late 1927, predating the book's publication by one to two years. In fact, however, the entire five-year period between 1925 and 1929 was devoted to the globetrotting that inspired not just *Hiver caraïbe*, but also accounts of travel in the near East, Asia, Africa and New York. It also yielded collections of travel-inspired stories, including one particularly significant work, *Magie noire*, based on the author's exploration of the American Deep South, the Caribbean and Africa (in that order). The second part of the 1920s was dedicated not just to the long expeditions themselves, but also to writing up, later on, the 'recollected' human and social, artistic and geographical discoveries. While Morand remained right up to the end of his life a compulsively productive writer, that frenetically peripatetic period saw him set out again and again to experience the wider world lying beyond Europe, not so much forensically, not with a direct focus on the past, but rather with a view to illuminating the present and future place of Europe – and of France more especially – in the global context.

---

4   Jeffrey Mehlman, 'French Literature and the Holocaust' in *Literature of the Holocaust*, ed. Alan Rosen, Cambridge: Cambridge University Press, 2013, p. 118.

Morand's Cultural Background

Morand was the privileged only child of highly cultured, artistically connected parents. His father, a painter and dramatist, but also a museum curator and later the distinguished director of the School of Decorative Arts in Paris, came from a French expatriate, industrialist background in Russia. In addition to benefiting from familial induction into the most exclusive Parisian cultural circles, young Paul Morand was not only educated in the best schools in Paris, but also spent some of his student days abroad: in Italy, where he often holidayed with his parents (Venice), but also in Spain and above all in England, both in London and in Oxford. Having taken first place in the competitive entrance exam or *concours* to the Ministry of Foreign Affairs, Morand entered the French diplomatic service in 1913. His early diplomatic career took him first to the capital cities of England, Spain and Italy and later on, in 1925 to an overseas posting in Bangkok.

Early Career

It might be thought that Paul Morand's early literary reputation was made more by his fiction than by his travel writing. In fact, however, even the early fiction is inspired and informed almost entirely by the author's cosmopolitan proclivities and by his exploration of 'other' places and cultures. His early literary success was not just inseparable from the jazzy atmosphere that lit up the *années folles* of the early 1920s; it was also remarkably Anglocentric in tenor.

Morand's most successful early works were short stories and these were based on his rather rarefied experience of life as a young, Anglophile diplomat in England. His first collection of short fiction, *Tendres stocks*, was published in 1921, while his second and third collections, *Ouvert la nuit* and *Fermé la nuit*, appeared in 1922 and 1923 respectively. On the basis of these stories, Morand was recognized from the start, both in England and in France, as a consummate stylist. This reputation, added to his powers of social observation, his privileged background and assiduous literary networking, made him a noted figure within the literary circles of his day. His highly urbane yet vivid writing was seen as having affinities, like that of Ezra Pound, with both the Modernist and Imagist aesthetics.

The most notable French author frequented by Morand at this time was Marcel Proust. Not only did the author of *À la recherche du temps perdu* support Morand both socially and in literary terms, but the young diplomat's first short-story collection was launched (in 1921) with a highly complimentary preface by Proust. Later on, Morand gravitated towards the most cosmopolitan and peripatetic of his contemporaries, although few of these would qualify as 'travel writers' per se. Some of them were fellow-diplomats: Paul Claudel, André Malraux and the 1960 Nobel laureate, Saint-John Perse (the pseudonym of Alexis Léger), all of whom had been posted to China for a number of years. Other notable traveller-writers whom Morand frequented were not, however, in the diplomatic service and these included André Gide and Valéry Larbaud.

Although Morand began his writing life as a career diplomat, he was most unconstrained by that professional or vocational structure. Having already taken time off to travel, to Morocco for example, while working for the foreign service in London, Morand quickly became definitively distracted not just from his day-job, but also from his overwhelmingly Anglophile focus on Europe. The narratives published in 1924 (the novel *Lewis et Irène*) and in 1925 (the stories of *L'Europe galante*) illustrate Morand's growing conviction that Europe was an exhausted world, in steep degenerative decline. This, then, was the spirit in which he conceived a fervid fascination with the potential for renewal associated with an exploration of the global East, West and South.

It was in 1925 that Morand's long-haul travel began in earnest. By 1927 it had reached such an intensity that, in the spring of that year, he embarked on a career break that would last some thirteen years, allowing him to devote himself fully to his top three interlinked priorities: writing, far-flung travel and socio-cultural elevation. In early January 1927, Morand married – in a civil and Greek Orthodox ceremony – Hélène Soutzo, a divorced socialite princess of Greco-Romanian origin whom he had met through Marcel Proust. She had been born in Trieste and was as snobbish as he was and probably more anti-Semitic. Despite his reputation as an inveterate womanizer, Morand remained winningly devoted to his wife up to and beyond the grave: their ashes today lie mingled in a tomb in Trieste.

A Eurocentric Traveller

Given that its author was a consummate European and fierce anti-communist, it is not surprising that Morand's entire oeuvre is marked by the rather lofty complacency of an Old-World sense of socio-cultural privilege and superiority. Yet this suave self-assurance is frequently undercut by a curiously perspicacious irony and even self-irony. Furthermore, the ethnocentric angle of Morand's perspective does not alter the fact that, from the mid-1920s to the early 1930s, his work testified – almost disarmingly – to a profoundly searching curiosity about other worlds and a wide-eyed, almost bulimic interest in human diversity. The world-wide scale of that orientation won for him the reputation of a globetrotter and sometime authority on the attractions and peculiarities, from an 'Über-European' perspective, of travel beyond Europe. Although he was drawn to Asia and Africa and wrote several books based on his travels there, he was particularly obsessed by the Americas, that intercontinental space of both African and European diaspora. And within that zone, which he had crisscrossed on several occasions, it was the truly concentrated crucible spaces of New York and the Caribbean that inspired his most impressive writing.

Reflecting on America

Morand's first encounter with America took place during what is often referred to as his 'world tour' of 1925. In June of that year, en route to his posting in Siam, he embarked at Cherbourg on the *Majestic*, travelling first to New York. He was particularly sensitive to the racial atmosphere of the city, as the Harlem Renaissance was at that point sparking intense interest in the cultural fallout of the African American history of transportation and plantation slavery. It was the vibrant charge of that electric American present, rather than the trauma or criminality of the American past that appears to have been of interest to Morand. Rather than pondering the historical and moral depths of the vast human migration experiment that combined genocidal European expansion into the 'New World' with mass transportation of African labour into the American plantations, he was held spellbound by the contemporary surface tension that was its legacy. This apparent deficit of attention to depth continued no matter how long Morand spent in the Americas or how many times he travelled there. In 1925, the year of his first visit to America, he only stayed a few weeks in New York before taking the scenic route to the Far East, crossing to the west coast of Canada, before setting sail, in the footsteps of Lafcadio Hearn[5] some thirty-five years previously, from Vancouver for Yokohama. He then travelled through Japan and into China, visiting Shanghai and Peking, before passing through Singapore to arrive at his final destination, Bangkok, at the beginning of September. After a few weeks in

---

5   Lafcadio Hearn, *Two Years in the French West Indies*, Oxford: Signal Books, 2001 [New York: Harpers, 1890]. Having lived for about twenty years in the US (in Cincinnati and New Orleans), Hearn spent almost two years in the Caribbean on a writing commission from *Harper's Magazine*: first on a Caribbean tour that yielded 'A Midsummer Trip to the Tropics' and then in Martinique specifically, a long sojourn that led to his 'Martinique Sketches'. Both works, published first in serial form in *Harper's Magazine*, were subsequently collected in the volume *Two Years*.

Siam he developed severe dysentery and was repatriated at the end of November via a clinic in Saigon. On this tour of the East he had met Paul Claudel (in China) and André Malraux (in Saigon).

Morand remained in Europe in 1926, touring Belgium and Holland in March of that year. He was, presumably, working on the Asian material that he had gathered in 1925, though he also appears to have visited the Museum of the Belgian Congo in Tervuren. In the course of 1926, the book based on his 1925 travels in the Far East, entitled *Rien que la terre* and subtitled 'Voyage', was published by Grasset. This work draws on Morand's first impressions of America and of Asia and its preface fully registers the writer's sense of global contraction: the world was becoming a smaller, less various place.

A series of further American sojourns followed in subsequent years, most notably two extensive trips in 1927. In all of Morand's travels, at least in so far as they find their way into his published writing, the focus, primarily aesthetic, is on the physical environment, both natural and built and on human diversity, both natural and socio-cultural. Moreover, the travel impressions usually inspired both fictional and non-fictional narratives. *Rien que la terre* launched the non-fiction cycle, initiating Morand's speculative and often prophetic reflection on the likely eventual creolization of the entire planet. This reflection is pursued with some considerable intensity in the non-fiction of the late 1920s: *A.O.F.*[6]: *de Paris à Tombouctou* (1928), *Hiver caraïbe* (1929) and *New York* (1930).

In parallel, and in near-perfect symmetry[7], Morand fulfilled the terms of the contract that he had agreed with Grasset for the publication of four short-story collections in a series entitled

---

6   A.O.F. stands for Afrique Occidentale Française (French West Africa). In subsequent editions, the title was shortened by the publisher (Ernest Flammarion) to *Paris-Tombouctou*.

7   The four-by-four symmetry is somewhat broken by the fact that Morand also published in 1927 a second volume of 'Far-Eastern' travel writing (tales set mostly in China). This was written directly in English, entitled *East India and Company*, and published in New York by Albert and Charles Boni in 1927.

Chroniques du XXe siècle. He was, indeed, along with a handful of other writers including François Mauriac, one of Grasset's most successful authors in the interwar years. The four volumes of fiction in of the series were: *L'Europe galante*, a collection set in, and centred on, Europe, which appeared in 1925; *Bouddha vivant*, a set of tales situated in Asia or based on an Asian view of Europe, also published in 1925; *Magie noire*, a suite of stories set in a triptych of locations – the southern states of the USA, the Caribbean and Africa. The fourth and final collection of the series was *Champions du monde* (published in 1930), featuring the stories of four athletes who had all been students together at Columbia University in New York.

Inspiration and Composition of Hiver caraïbe

If one were to believe the chronology and itinerary of the journey recounted in *Hiver caraïbe*, one would gather that, early in the winter of 1927, Morand set off all alone from France on a voyage to and around the Caribbean. This trip, readers were to believe, took him first to Guadeloupe and Martinique and then (in order) to Trinidad, Venezuela, Curaçao, Haiti, Jamaica, Cuba and finally right through Mexico, up into California as far as Los Angeles. In fact, however, Morand made not one, but two successive journeys to the Americas in 1927, the first beginning in January, the second in November. He then let his impressions of the two trips crystallize for between one and two years before re-writing several aspects of his travels, passing off the last stage of the first trip as the last part of the second one and fictionalizing or at least massaging certain other circumstances of his itineraries. Above all, he fleshed out his travel notes with many long, reflective disquisitions on topics of particular interest to him.

Readers of Morand were afforded access to these secrets after his manuscript notes for the travelogue were found by chance in 2010 in the archives of the Académie Française by a researcher,

Dominique Lanni, who was investigating Morand's encounter in Haiti with the novelist Jacques Roumain. The notebook in which Morand had written his Caribbean impressions was transcribed and annotated by Dr Lanni[8], who has produced an invaluable forensic comparison of the apparently contemporaneous impressions, on the one hand, and on the other, the published text. This analysis reveals not just how Morand worked, but also the full extent of his re-casting of his impressions for publication.

The truth is that, in late January 1927, less than three weeks after his wedding on January 3rd, Morand undertook, not alone, but rather along with his wife Hélène, an extensive tour that brought him, to begin with, aboard the liner *L'Espagne* from Saint-Nazaire in France to Havana in Cuba and thence to Veracruz in Mexico. After travelling extensively through Mexico, the couple proceeded up into California before undertaking a road trip from the west coast right across to the east coast of the United States, a voyage that ended, after some protracted exploration of Louisiana and of Georgia, in New York. The Morands then returned to France. In March of the same year, Morand's career break from the diplomatic service was officially approved; his avowed intention was to use this hiatus to 'study intellectual relations between France and America'[9]. In line with this transcontinental project, he set off once again for the Americas in November 1927, again along with his wife Hélène, sailing this time from Bordeaux to the Caribbean. This next transatlantic trip followed the trajectory recalled and recorded as a bachelor's adventure in the first two thirds of *Hiver caraïbe*. It brought the couple first to Guadeloupe and Martinique, then to Trinidad, Venezuela and Curaçao, before taking them to the three largest islands of the Caribbean: to Haiti and Jamaica, first, and then on the morning of December 20th, to Cuba, more

---

8   Paul Morand, *Carnets d'un voyage aux Antilles, Haïti/Jamaïque/ Cuba, nov.-déc. 1927*, ed. with an Introduction by Dominique Lanni, 'Vagabondages', Paris: Editions Passage(s), 2016.

9   See D. Lanni's introduction to Paul Morand, *Carnets, op. cit.*, p.193.

specifically Santiago de Cuba. The entry for December 22nd records Morand's arrival in Havana and explicitly mentions the fact that this is the writer's second visit to the Cuban port, since he had already stayed there eleven months earlier. The entry for December 23rd is the last dated entry in the book. It announces the departure on December 24th of the boat that will take, Morand announces, two full days to make the crossing to Veracruz in Mexico.

Only the informed reader knows that Morand's announced crossing from Cuba to Mexico was effected not in the last days of 1927 but rather in the first weeks of that same year, and that the entire section on Mexico is based on recollections of that earlier, honeymoon trip. So while the manuscript version of the diary does indeed end with impressions of Cuba, just prior to departure to the American mainland, the Morands' second Caribbean visit ended with a crossing not to Mexico but to Louisiana. This (second) stay in Louisiana was followed by a tour of Georgia, Alabama, Mississippi, North and South Carolina and Virginia, before the couple eventually ended their second American journey of 1927, as they had ended the first one, in New York, whence they embarked for Europe.

A Triangular Focus: Europe-Africa-America

All of Morand's 1920s American writings privilege the fundamentally triangular relation between Europe, Africa and the Americas. Indeed, what lies at the heart of these works is an emphasis on the transatlantic diaspora: not just the European colonization of the Americas, but also the associated mass transportation of African slaves both to the continent and to the Caribbean. That emphasis is particularly visible in the table of contents of *Magie noire*, which is divided into three sections: *Antilles, Etats-Unis d'Amérique* and *Afrique*. Interestingly, the American translation inverts the order of the first two sections, putting the US stories first. In both versions, however, Africa comes last and this reflects the fact that Morand's grand tour of Africa (Morocco, Senegal, Guinea and Mali) only took place in 1928. The stories of *Magie noire* were published in book form in June 1928, while *Paris-Tombouctou*, the African travelogue, appeared at the end of October 1928. In January 1929, Morand returned to New York, where he probably worked on the manuscript of *New York*, a work that appeared in December 1929 in the *Revue de Paris* and then in book form with Grasset in 1930. So although New York had been Morand's principal African American port of call in the 1920s, and although he stayed there on at least four occasions, his account of his impressions of the city was thus the very last of the three 'African American' non-fiction volumes to make its way into print.

A Thorn in the Side of Post-War France

After the sustained travelling and writing frenzy of the 1925-1930 period, Morand's literary productivity may have slowed down somewhat, but he did continue right through the 1930s to publish many works of both fiction and non-fiction, including travel books on the cities of London and Bucharest. However, his days of intercontinental travel and of far-flung travel-based writing appear to have petered out completely by the mid-1930s.[10] 1938, the year of Morand's return to the diplomatic service – or the 'Carrière' as it was called in French – was a most inauspicious one for Europe. Morand was appointed to a position in London as the head of a commission charged with restricting the German Reich's freedom of movement at sea, a post in which he was would have been well placed to ally

---

10 Morand's non-fiction based on travel outside Europe included two works published in the 1930s: *Air Indien*, on South America, which was published in 1932 and translated by Desmond Flower as *Indian Air: Impressions of Travel in South America*, London: Cassell, 1933 and *La Route des Indes*, on the Near East, which was published by Plon in 1936.

himself with resistance to fascism. Yet he turned away from this smile of fortune, confirming instead his identification with the collaborationist Vichy government, which he proceeded to serve in diplomatic postings to Bucharest and Bern. Morand later 'explained' this move to his friends as having been prompted by his need to humour his imperious, Germanophile wife who felt out of place in the 'Free France' atmosphere of London. As a result of this collaboration, he was stripped, following the Liberation of France, both of his mission and of his pension. Correctly understanding that he was persona non grata in his home country, he settled in Switzerland, dividing his time between Vevey on the shore of Lake Geneva and Tangiers in Morocco.

Inevitably, Morand was regarded as a political pariah after the war; and, predictably, his literary reputation was almost entirely erased by his disgrace. This fate compares very favourably, of course, with that of more clearly fascist-leaning collaborationist writers: Robert Brasillach, for example, who was executed in February 1945, or Pierre Drieu de la Rochelle, who took his own life in March of the same year. Indeed, Morand's sentence was, to all appearances, held to have been fully served in 1955, when he was accepted back into the French diplomatic service, although he almost immediately retired. Emboldened no doubt by this highly symbolic professional rehabilitation, he repeated (thrice) his first unsuccessful attempt to be elected to the French Academy. Neither he nor his supporters were in the least deterred by the repeated political roadblocks put in his way, including the personal veto of General de Gaulle. He was eventually admitted to a seat amongst the so-called 'Immortels' on his fourth attempt, in 1968. Although Morand's longevity was the major, and perhaps even the sole, reason for his eventual return from the cold, it is true that, for better reasons than those adduced by some of his supporters, notably the group called the *Hussards*, which included Roger Nimier, the literary establishment could not indefinitely pretend that his writings did not exist or that they merited neither critical attention nor literary acclaim.

Certainly, as a writer who did not avoid talking the talk of casual (and at times far worse than casual) racism, and who never saw fit to distance himself, however belatedly, from the eugenic and genocidal agenda that conclusively annihilated Europe's (self-)image as civilization's standard-bearer and humanity's beacon in the twentieth century, Morand represents, on a scale almost comparable to Louis-Ferdinand Céline, an incurable headache for French culture. It is difficult to regard the ill-borne delay in his nomination to the Academy as proportionate reparation for his lifelong failure to repudiate his racist statements and his collaborationist positions. Nonetheless, his precocious literary talent, cosmopolitan cultural flair and acute, even prophetic perspective on Europe's (future) place in the world are impossible to deny and difficult to ignore. Moreover, it is precisely the complicated and cautionary cohabitation of these strengths with the throwaway racism that was so much of his time and so very close to the heart of darkness, that requires of our own challenged age more rather than less critical attention.

If Morand's profile never really recovered from the war-time nosedive of judgement, his disgrace seems to have had little or no effect on his self-belief or literary energy, which never seemed to fail him. He thus continued, both when he was out in the cold and when he came back into the cultural fold, to publish both fiction and non-fiction at a most sustained pace. He also retained his passion for racing, expressed most notably in his fondness for horses, swimming and fast cars. Despite this apparent continuity, Morand's non-fiction and even some of his fictional work underwent a 'historical turn' in the post-war years. Increasingly, he pondered the past, writing a biography of Maupassant, for example, and a dramatic work about Isabeau of Bavaria, the tragic wife of King Charles VI. Curiously, this latter work was translated into English by the renowned travel-writer Patrick Leigh Fermor, although the publisher John Murray, whom Fermor tried to interest in the project, does not seem to have been keen to publish the English version. The historically focused work also includes books on the Spanish Inquisition and on the Spanish Civil War. It further provides one possible indication of Morand's sensitivity to public perception of his choices. For, as one critic has pointed out, several of these later, historically-based essays centre on the collision between the destiny of one exceptional individual on the one hand, and complicated political situations, on the other.[11]

Morand's overall literary trajectory raises one very obvious question that is of central relevance to the place of *Hiver caraïbe* in his oeuvre as a whole. His eager discussion in all of his 1920s writings of various pseudoscientific ideas on race, racial hierarchies and miscegenation may not be to his credit, but they are inscribed within a genuinely searching intellectual engagement. The focus of Morand's engagement with these ideas is less on the viability of the 'Old World' and of its values than on the shape and the colour of the world or worlds to come. Some of the issues that he raises in this connection are quite impressive in their lucidity and prescience: for example, the question of an economically but also climatically motivated movement of mass migration from the southern hemisphere. Yet given that Morand could have stress-tested throughout the troubled 1930s and cataclysmic 1940s all the ideas that he had explored in his 1920s American cycle, why did he fail to re-visit these in the light of

---

11   See Kimberly Philpot van Noort, *Paul Morand: the Politics and Practice of Writing in Post-War France*, Amsterdam: Rodopi, 2001, on Morand's postwar studies of historical losers, whom he tends to present as falling foul of an impersonal Destiny as much as – if not more than – of individual failings or blindness. An example of his predilection for excavating exceptional individual destinies in politically complicated historical contexts would be his study of Louis XIV's ill-fated minister, Fouquet: *Fouquet, ou le soleil offusqué* (Fouquet, or the Offended Sun), published in 1961.

subsequent events? Furthermore, Morand had the advantage of living a long and healthy life that extended right through the 1945-54 war of decolonization of 'French Indochina' and then through the decolonization of 'French Africa' in the 1950s and 1960s and of the entire Caribbean too, at least in name, with the exception of France's three enduring possessions. Why, in the face of this extraordinary political ferment, not to mention the civil rights movement that eventually swept over the USA, did Morand remain silent on so many of the real and crucial questions (migration, racial discrimination, cultural diversity, socialism, etc.) that had exercised him in the 1920s? Why, in particular, was his interest in the transatlantic triangle so spectacularly short-lived?

Any response to this question would have to take into account the general lack of European engagement in Morand's life-time with the issues and ideas raised in or by his 'African-American' work. The fact is that the 'old continent' suffered two acute seizures in the 1940s and 1960s. The toxic shock waves that they propagated seem to have produced a profound and chilling effect on open, free and lucid critique. It was only in the 1980s that postcolonial studies and related approaches began to open up a space for such thinking in and around Europe.

Morand's Reception: the Case of Hiver caraïbe

Although the Caribbean was central to the dynamic of reverse cross-fertilization whereby Africa and its diffractive American diaspora began to affect Europe in return, the status of the Caribbean and of the Americas in general as a laboratory of creolization was not widely appreciated in the 1920s. Despite the work of prophetic writers like Lafcadio Hearn and Paul Morand, the significance of the Creole world would only start to be glimpsed when the high winds of anti-colonialism eventually inspired incendiary works like the *Cahier d'un retour au pays natal*

(Notebook of a Return to the Native Land)[12] by the Martinican writer, Aimé Césaire. This work, which was published in 1939, was 'discovered' by André Breton when he set foot in Martinique in 1941, a literary encounter that is often seen as launching the process by which Caribbean voices began to reverberate and register in France.

It would not be surprising if, given the relative lack of sociological or cultural interest during the 1920s and 1930s in Europe's plantation colonies, which were not yet recognized as having a 'social destiny' or a 'culture' to speak of, *Hiver caraïbe* received relatively less attention (both in Europe and in the US) than did Morand's related writings on the African diaspora in New York. In fact, however, at roughly the same time as Morand was publishing his flurry of 'black magic' works, the publishing house Mercure de France was bringing out French translations of Lafcadio Hearn's extensive Caribbean writings, translations authored by the prolific translator Marc (Mary-Cécile) Logé, who was also translating Agatha Christie. This early translation is perhaps proof of precocious French interest in the Caribbean in the 1920s and early 1930s. It seems, however, that this attention fizzled out or went underground during the lead-up to the war and during the first three post-war decades (referred to in France as the *trente glorieuses* of reconstruction). In other words, neither Hearn's nor Morand's Caribbean writings were to any significant extent disinterred during the 1950s and 1960s, even though the tidal waves of decolonization, most notably the Indochina and Algerian wars, were beginning to make it clear that post-colonial fallout was going to be one of France's biggest challenges for the best part of a century. Indeed, the ever-increasing visibility and ever-gathering potency of that fallout may at least partly explain why, from the late 1980s onwards, there was eventually a move away from France's post-war boycotting of Morand's work.

---

12 Aimé Césaire's epic poem was first published in a journal in 1939: *Volontés*, no. 20, 1939, pp. 23-51.

In 1988, over a decade after Morand's death (in Paris during the 1976 summer heatwave), Flammarion published a new edition of *New York*, complete with a most laudatory preface by the contemporary novelist and literary critic, Philippe Sollers. In this introductory piece, Sollers identifies Morand as one of the three most important French writers of the twentieth century, placing him on a par both with Céline and with Proust. Not only that, but he goes on to single out *Hiver caraïbe* as one of Morand's most interesting works. Then, fifteen years later, in 1991, Flammarion brought out a new edition of *Hiver caraïbe*. The engaging preface to the new edition was written by the novelist and French academician, Michel Déon, who belonged to the anti-existentialist, right-wing group called the *Hussards*, who had been instrumental in Morand's eventual literary rehabilitation.

Although Sollers' salute dates from the late 1980s, this writer has continued to follow closely the renewal of interest in Morand in France. He has reviewed, for example, successive volumes of Morand's correspondence, which is currently being published by degrees by Gallimard. Morand's literary will had stipulated that these 'private' writings would not be published until after 2000. So far, the correspondence with Roger Nimier, Alain Chambord and others has appeared to significant specialist and general interest. Naturally, the drip-feed, posthumous publication of the writer's uninhibited expression of his ideas, including his prejudices, and in particular his anti-Semitic and homophobic inclinations, has been very effective in putting Morand under the spotlight in France. This spike of critical attention has, predictably, resulted in turn in new editions of several important studies in French, both of the author and of his writing,[13] and it has also added further significance and resonance to the work of those critics and

---

13 For example, Ginette Guitard-Auviste, *Paul Morand (1888-1976), légendes et vérités*, Paris: Hachette, 1981; this work was brought out in a new edition by Balland in 1994.

scholars who had already been taking an interest in Morand's writings, including *Hiver caraïbe*.[14]

Flammarion and Gallimard are not the only publishers who are currently contributing to the rise in Morand's stock. Grasset is, as one would expect, also very involved in this remarkable renewal of literary and critical interest, bringing out a new edition of *Magie noire* in the spring of 2016. More recently still, in June 2016, a new publisher, Passage(s), riding on the same propitious wind, made available in its 'Vagabondages' series the notes taken by Morand on his Caribbean journey (notes that, as we have already seen, had been gathering dust in the archives of the Académie Française).

Morand in English

Paradoxically perhaps, the aspects of Morand's work that would appear to be of most interest to the English-speaking world today are less the works with a 'global', transcontinental perspective than those that foreground the Anglocentric or hyper-European aesthetic. This was not always so absolutely the case, however.

It was for a British publisher, Chapman and Dodd, that Ezra Pound was very swiftly commissioned to translate two of Morand's earliest story collections, both set in London and thus of considerable specific interest to English readers: *Tendres stocks* (1921), a title that Pound rendered as *Fancy Goods*) and *Ouvert la nuit* (1922, translated as *Open All Night*). However, Pound's translation was ultimately deemed too risqué to be printed by Chapman and Dodd; certainly his translation of the first allusive title – which referred to English women – does indicate a certain

---

14 For astute commentary on some of Morand's statements in *Hiver caraïbe* see, for example, Elizabeth Ezra, *The Colonial Unconscious*, Ithaca NY: Cornell University Press, 2000. See also Kimberly Philpot van Noort, *Paul Morand: the Politics and Practice of Writing in Post-War France, op. cit.*.

freedom and directness of approach. To resolve their dilemma, Chapman and Dodd proceeded to commission a different translator, one H.I. Woolf, to produce a tamer version of *Tendres stocks*, which duly appeared in 1923 as *Green Shoots*. The too-hot-to-handle Pound translations were handed over to William Bird, the founder of Three Mountains Press, based in Paris. Nothing came of this approach, however, and Pound's version of the stories seems to have been shelved and forgotten about. In the mid-1970s it surfaced again in Virginia in the US and about ten years later, a press called New Directions, based in New York, brought out Pound's translations of Morand's first two story collections in one volume, complete with Proust's original preface.

The 'World Writing' in Translation

Paul Morand himself had excellent English, so much so that, as already noted, he wrote one of his travel-based fictional works, a story collection entitled *East India Company*, directly in English. This translingual tour de force was (tellingly) published, not in London, but in New York in 1927 by Alfred and Charles Boni. It was first translated into French by Béatrice Vierne and published under the same title in Paris in 1987 by Arléa. Almost none of the French-language works based on Morand's travels had to wait sixty weeks, much less sixty years, to be translated into English. However, these translations were almost all published in the US. The story collection, *Magie noire* (1928), was immediately translated into English, as was *New York* (1930), by Hamish Miles for the American publisher, Viking Press: *Black Magic* appeared in late 1929 and the English version of *New York* in 1930. Given the predominantly US focus of these two works, it is no accident that they were the ones to be commissioned by US rather than British publishers. Similarly, the English version of Morand's 1926 Asia-based travel report, *Rien que la terre* was translated by Lewis Galantière (as *Nothing but the Earth*) and published in November 1927 by the New York-based press, R.M. McBride & Co.

What is perhaps surprising is that there have been no new editions of these American translations and that no new translations been commissioned to refresh the 1920 versions. Given the renewed level of contemporary interest in France in Morand's post-colonial reflections on New World culture, on the African diaspora and on world race-relations, and given, in particular, the re-launching in the late twentieth and early twenty-first centuries of the original French versions of *Black Magic* and *New York*, it is even more astonishing that there has been no interest in translating *Hiver caraïbe*. This neglect is all the more remarkable given the millennial translation renaissance enjoyed by other works by Morand. After all, a *third* English translation of *Tendres stocks*, this time by Euan Cameron, was published in London in 2011 by the Pushkin Press (under the title *Tender Shoots*). It might appear that this rebirth of English interest in Morand is prompted by the close association between Morand's very early literary fiction and his Anglophilia. However, the lie is given to that interpretation by the fact that Pushkin has also published the first English translation of four other, much later works by Morand, works in which the author's early fixation on England had considerably faded. In 2009, Pushkin issued the first English translation (by David Coward) of the 1954 novel of feminine sexual depravity, set in Tangiers: *Hecate and her Dogs*. And then the press released translations, all by Euan Cameron, of three further works, two of which are non-fiction: in 2009, *The Allure of Chanel* (the French original had appeared in 1976); in 2013, *Venices* (the original had been published in 1971); and in 2015, *The Man in a Hurry* (the translation of a 1941 novel).

As the above summary makes clear, the afterlife of Morand's work in recent English translation is largely confined to the European register of the oeuvre. It thereby avoids completely the question of racial difference that lies at the heart of *Hiver caraïbe* and more generally of the 'African American' writings. It is tempting to speculate on the reasons behind the exclusion of this corpus from the millennial renewal of interest in Morand within the English-language translation repertoire. It is certainly possible that the racialist tenor of this body of work has been seen as casting too dark a shadow on the work of an author already tarnished by his association with anti-Semitism and collaborationism. In addition, Morand's provocative style, so detached and ironic, may make it all but unreadably anachronistic on certain topics, such as miscegenation or economic migration.

If, then, it has taken Paul Morand's travel journal, *Hiver caraïbe*, ninety years to be translated into English, this is probably not because it counts as a minor composition, or as undeserving of the interest and attention associated with translation into English. Quite to the contrary, its condemnation for so long to the purdah of non-translation is probably best explained by the fact that it is part of Morand's most potent and pungent corpus, a corpus that Anglophone Europe was not at all ready to face when it first appeared, and that Anglophone America was interested in at the time, but only in so far as it had a direct bearing on the United States themselves, rather than on their Caribbean backyard.

Morand's Perspective on the Caribbean

The manuscript notebook in which Morand sketched out his travel impressions in diary form includes a section (under the heading 'Preface') in which he gives the rationale for his project. These statements are not included in the published work but they give a most instructive insight into Morand's perspective in *Hiver caraïbe*. The preface opens with a demographical observation about the '200 million Negroes' in the world's population, and then goes on to reference the 'importing' of Blacks to the USA, the Caribbean and Brazil. Morand predicts that his book will please 'neither Negrophobes nor Negrophiles', neither 'Whites nor Blacks'. He next proceeds to divide the Whites into two groups: 'Anglo-Saxon [*sic*] racists and the rest, including the French, who are faithful to [the spirit of] the eighteenth-century Enlightenment and to the French Revolution'. He notes that, for the latter, humans are everywhere the same ('[ils] pensent que l'homme est partout le même').[15] Both perspectives, he argues, are misguided and lead to error. Yet his own largely evolutionist view seems to be quite muddled. He states that Blacks are 'still children and won't face facts'; that they are 'not superior to us [*sic*]' but that progress can work 'miracles'. Arguing that any attempt to assimilate Blacks and Whites would be a disastrous mistake, he concludes that the same kinds of inequalities exist between different races as between different individuals, even though he adds that the brutality of this 'natural law' can and should be softened.

The particular significance of *Hiver caraïbe* is not just, as already suggested, that it reveals so much about Morand's articulated thinking and about his unthinking reflexes on major questions. Firstly, it helps us to build up a more complete and complex portrait of the way the triangular time-space of all of African America was conceptualized in Europe in the interwar years. Secondly, it elucidates the moral and intellectual confusion and complexity of late 1920s European pseudoscientific thought on, or fantasizing about, 'racial' identity, diversity and inequality. Thirdly, it is extraordinarily prescient in its adumbration of so many of the principal on-going challenges of our own age: these include the meaning and the future of ethnic and national diversity and relationality; the conundrum of democracy in a shrinking world, more especially the struggle between socialism and capitalism in the new intercontinental world order; the desire to control mass economic migration and the policing of borders.

---

15 Again, Dominique Lanni's archival work is the source of this invaluable information on Morand's perspective on his Caribbean project. See Paul Morand, *Carnets d'un voyage aux Antilles, op. cit.*, pp. 35-6.

CARIBBEAN WINTER

From Lafcadio Hearn to Paul Morand

The subtitle originally given to *Hiver caraïbe* is 'documentaire' and this provides a clue to its crypto-journalistic status in Morand's eyes as reportage. Indeed, he gave his work the same diary form as Lafcadio Hearn's island-hopping 'A Midsummer Trip to the Tropics', published in 1889 in serial form by *Harper's Magazine* and later on, in 1890, as the first section of a book entitled *Two Years in the French West Indies*. Given this convergence of genre and perspective, and given his intense interest in the Caribbean crucible, it is not surprising that Morand had read Lafcadio Hearn's work, nor that he quotes from it on several occasions in *Hiver caraïbe*. The greater part of Hearn's volume, a section entitled 'Martinique Sketches', had been translated into French and published in two volumes by the Mercure de France in 1924 and 1926. The shorter section, focusing on the Caribbean journey as a whole (the aforementioned 'Midsummer Trip to the Tropics') was not translated into French until 1931. However, Morand read and wrote English fluently and would have been well able to read Hearn in the original.

Much more than forty years separate the two perspectives on the Caribbean, the two sensibilities and the two styles. First of all, Morand's Caribbean travel diary gives way in the final third of the book to an unbroken account of the author's continental journey up through Mexico to California. Hearn's 'Midsummer Trip' similarly gives way to his 'Martinique Sketches'. However, although both works move away from the travel diary form, many of Hearn's 'Martinique Sketches' take the form of folktales or short stories. Morand's writing in *Hiver caraïbe* is, on the contrary, exclusively essayistic and anecdotal and never segues into fictional narrative. Like Hearn's travel diary, *Hiver caraïbe* offers typically taut and often quirky geographical, cultural, aesthetic and sociological observation, but unlike Hearn's reportage, Morand's entries are interspersed with gripping passages of frank, even extreme 'opinionation' on very big philosophical or political questions. Moreover, while Hearn's attention is perhaps just as fixated as Morand's on the question of racial difference, Morand's focus is less aesthetic and more speculative and political than Hearn's.

If the gap between the two perspectives is more than merely chronological, it is only partly for the reasons just outlined. For it is also and perhaps in great part due to the dramatic distance separating the authors' backgrounds. Morand came to the Caribbean as a privileged, cosmopolitan French dandy, a continental European dazzled by his sense of his own (racy rather than jaded), quintessentially French, Old-World superiority, a superiority already tried and tested in the most sophisticated capital cities of the world: London, Venice, New York... Hearn, on the other hand, was – at the time of his encounter with the Caribbean – an American immigrant from a multiply displaced, migrant, colonial, archipelagic and mixed background (he was of Greco-Anglo-Irish origin). He had been abandoned in Dublin by both parents as a very small child and was brought up there by a paternal grand-aunt, before she too packed him off to boarding-school in England. The orphaned child grew up to be a rootless or at least homeless nomad, a marginal, a serial misfit, but also an unconditional Francophile, who was able to bring his own experience of marginality and homelessness, along with his obvious gift of cultural empathy, to bear upon a lifetime of storytelling. Hearn pushed his interest in the stories of African America to the point of contracting an illegal marriage in Cincinnati with a freed Kentucky slave. Having come to the Caribbean via his role as an embedded reporter in the black ghettoes of Cincinnati and via an immersive Creole apprenticeship in New Orleans, he viewed this space and its people from an entirely different perspective to that of the polished and urbane, *über*-French diplomat-dandy. And yet both writers were equally fascinated by the Caribbean crucible, correctly recognizing it as infinitely portentous in terms of the future of what we now call post-colonial humanity.

Hiver caraïbe is compelling reading largely because of the concentrated (if often self-contradictory) intelligence of many of its insights and observations and for the punchiness of its style. Despite the tensions and dissonance in Morand's thinking, his attempt to think through the realities and likely legacy of colonialism and of creolization is often arresting. For example, despite his use of terms like 'half-caste' and his derogatory remarks on those whom he so offensively characterizes as such, and despite his characteristic failure to follow through properly on his pithy insights, he is able to recognize that ' those who mingle and mix will detest one another, but at least they won't come to blows.'[16] He also recognizes that the reason for US hegemony in the Caribbean basin is that 'states of hybrid composition, stripped of their indigenous races' can expect no fate other than 'serial colonization'[17]. This is the fate that he wants France to avoid by closing its borders to all save those identifiable as Celts...

The Long Continental Coda of Hiver caraïbe

One of the most intriguing questions raised by the structure and focus of *Hiver caraïbe* concerns the work's very long continental coda. As we have seen, Morand positions the Mexican-Californian interlude at the end of his Caribbean adventure, whereas this adventure had ended in reality with an extensive tour of the Deep South states, beginning with Louisiana. How should we interpret this monumental discrepancy between the actual itinerary of Morand's Caribbean travels and the published record? This deviation raises a further, related question that also invites speculation, namely the subject matter that Morand

---

16   See below, p. 110.
17   See below, pp.109-110.

neglected to report on. Why did he not find the American 'Deep South', particularly perhaps Louisiana, worth dwelling on? Why, instead of writing up his travels in the 'deep southern' states, did he choose to replace that subject with his impressions of Mexico and California?

The answers to these questions are perhaps implicit in the work itself. It is possible that the southern states were in 1927 still too swamped – for Morand's comfort – in the timeless rural farmland torpor that succeeded their slave-plantation past, a social narcosis that he had had no difficulty overlooking in his whirlwind tour of a series of very diverse Caribbean islands. After all, what Morand's Caribbean narrative offers are fast-paced, virtuoso sketches of one island city or town after another and it highlights in particular the very diverse electric charges of the various island capitals. Furthermore, during the author's occasional sorties into the rural hinterland of Caribbean urban centres, he always seem to make for the aesthetic ether of the islands' sub-tropical highlands.

This later gravitation is entirely consonant with the Morand's Mexican-Californian diversion. As the last third of *Hiver caraïbe* clearly shows, his substitution of the continental code for the interminable plantation flatlands of the Deep South expanses allowed him to sustain his determined embrace of the American sublime. In other words, the deviation to a central and south-western focus made it possible for Morand to cross with no drop in intensity from the volcanic intensity of the Caribbean to the epic majesty of those continental vistas, as materialized in the vast empty plains and in the dizzying relief and altitude of the Mexican and Californian desert landscapes.

It is, of course, one of the ironies and contradictions of Morand's thinking that his impressions of urban life in the various Caribbean ports and his gravitation towards the socio-cultural and political worlds of the elites based in the various capitals brought him right into the throbbing heartland, into the very epicentre of the irremediably blended, mixed-race world that he so often affected to despise, whereas his Deep South sojourns must have offered him unlimited opportunities to savour the apotheosis of that respect for racial distinctions that he on occasion categorically preached. Certainly, the time that he spent in the Deep South, far more effectively than any of his other travels, in Europe, the Caribbean, east or west coast of the USA or Africa, must have allowed him to see first-hand what racial segregation or apartheid meant in practice. Is it any wonder that he averted his gaze? In this reading, then, the Mexican and Californian deflection allowed Morand to sustain the high notes of the simmering Caribbean score, without having to 'face facts' about the logical implications of his murky ruminations on and around the matter of race. More specifically it distracted him and his reader from the manner in which this matter was being played out in the white supremacism and segregation of the American South.

One further explanation of the Mexican-Californian deviation is worth considering. As one astute critic has noted, Paul Morand's pre-war writings are not much concerned with history.[18] Certainly, in the Caribbean, Morand's perspective is much more synchronic than diachronic. In fact, though, regardless of his own an-historical disposition, historiographical and *a fortiori* pre-historiographical depth is utterly frustrated in the Caribbean by the completeness on all the islands of the aboriginal genocide and ethnocide. And indeed Morand does explicitly acknowledge in *Hiver caraïbe* this annihilation of the indigenous peoples of the Caribbean.[19] In this context, we could perhaps read the Mexican and

---

18 Kimberly Philpot van Noort observes that, after the war, Morand's writing undergoes an 'almost total turn towards historical fiction and non-fiction', p. 10. See Kimberly Philpot van Noort, *Paul Morand: the Politics and Practice of Writing in Post-War France, op.cit.*, p.10.

19 See below, pp. 107, 109, 113.

Californian deviation as implicitly and retrospectively allowing the historical-cultural emptiness and muteness of the Antillean landscape to resonate by contrasting it with the eloquence of pre-Columbian remains and vestiges in Mexico. Whether or not this was a conscious or unconscious effort to compensate for the occlusive European eradication of the historical and pre-historical depth of the Caribbean, it is a fact that most of Morand's Mexican commentary is either centred on, or regularly punctuated by, reflection on the (still) eloquently visible man-made vestiges of the Mayan and Aztec civilizations.

Paul Morand's Caribbean narrative ends with a few lyrical lines on the Pacific Ocean, lying in repose on the western seaboard, as far away from the transatlantic crime scene as it is possible to be without leaving the Americas entirely. And yet the penultimate paragraphs of *Hiver caraïbe* are haunted by the demeaning of multiple peoples and their worlds right across the Americas from north to south and from east to west, an ongoing desecration that Morand was able to see for himself. Unsettling the image of the apparently pacified ocean to which the author has travelled on an old Apache trail, the pathetic echoes of the war chants of four Navajo elders bear witness to the legions of the native disappeared. The final image of *Hiver caraïbe* is of a 'ghostly' or 'spectral' ocean. Yet the ghosts that haunt this work as a whole are not just the ghosts of indigenous Americans or First Nations, but also the ghosts of those whose bones lie on the floor of the other ocean, along with the spirits of those whose bodies did survive the Middle Passage, only to suffer through several generations the 'social death' of transatlantic slavery. In that sense, the phantom presence of other spaces, other times and other stories inevitably hovers around Morand's narrative. And it is precisely in turning his face away from that presence that he allows it to make itself so tellingly felt.

Translator's Note

It is not easy to render what one critic has so aptly identified as the 'brittle polish'[20] of Morand's voice, that distinctive timbre that is such a crucial part of his message: quick-fire, elegant and knowing, but often elliptical, even ambiguous. In addition to this stylistic challenge, there is the difficulty posed by Morand's terminological inconsistency. He seems, for example, to use the words *nègre* and *noir* quite interchangeably. Furthermore, when using them as nouns, to refer to persons, he sometimes, but not always, capitalizes these terms, following the French spelling rule for nouns identifying individuals by their nationality or ethnicity ('une Française', 'les Anglais' etc.). The word *Nègre* has been translated as 'Negro', *Noir* as 'Black' and *Blanc* as 'White', and the English terms have always been capitalized when they refer to persons. In other words, Morand's language has not been sanitized or camouflaged in any way. On the contrary, since capitalization has been applied more consistently in the translation than in the original, the effect is to highlight Morand's obsession with, or belief in, the idea, the value and the stability of racial identifiers based on binary distinctions.

The translator gratefully acknowledges the invaluable support, moral and practical, that the project received from J.M.G. Le Clézio, James Ferguson of Signal Books, Patricia Palmer of Maynooth University, the National University of Ireland and, in the final stages, from Tora Kelly.

---

20 Richard Sieburth, 'A New Voice from the 1920s', in *The New York Times*, June 17th 1984. This article is a review of Pound's translations for New Directions Press.

CARIBBEAN WINTER

NOVEMBER 9TH, 1927

This morning three men burst into my room. From my bed I watch them stick red, white and blue labels on my luggage, then haul it away on their backs. The next time I'll see my trunks they will be in my cabin on board the ship.

My eyes linger one last time on the straight lines of the furniture, on the horizontal tracks of the parquet flooring and the steady window frame. I savour their stability. From this moment on, until we reach the West Indies, everything will be in motion.

Tomorrow afternoon I set sail from Bordeaux, so today is my last day in Paris. On the eve of a departure the aim must be to live as if one were not on the verge of leaving, as if one were the most settled of those who stay put. But how can I forget that tomorrow I shall no longer be here? Like someone set on taking his own life that very evening, a man facing imminent departure can imagine he's the master of his own life.

NOVEMBER 10TH

Bordeaux, 7 a.m. The sickly early-morning light is a symphony in grey and there's a wind from the north-west. With the newspapers forecasting a hurricane due to spread from the Channel to Morocco, I'm overcome by a violent urge not to leave after all. This is the time for being struck by faint-heartedness. I recall how a youthful Robinson Crusoe was turned off adventure the instant the first storm hit the coast of England. All he wanted was to return to his father's house but he didn't dare. It's this apprehension, this fear of running home that underlies all the exploits of Defoe's hero.

It's 4 p.m. now and the *Flandre*[21] has docked. All thirteen thousand tons of her. How very moving it is, that instant of initial encounter between passenger and liner, that first intersection of their respective destinies!

The clientele is neither as wealthy nor as lucrative as on the Cuba-Mexico line. But it's more exotic, with throngs of coloureds in second and third class. The ship's belly is bursting with merchandise, which promises stability at sea. Rain has come in from the West, pouring warm water into the cornucopia of the Gironde basin, while off in the distance autumn has tinted the hills with henna.

And so there it is, the fleet of the CGT.[22] Its vessels are all lying at ease. Lined up in the estuary, they bear the red and black chimneys so often glimpsed out at sea. It's a landscape of masts and barrels, of farewells on the sloping drawbridge, of decks almost genuflecting onto the pier, of bales of cotton and beautiful Creoles wearing copper earrings. The ships resemble those old vessels bound for the colonies, the ones depicted on Bordeaux wood engravings from the heyday of the triangular trade and of Monsieur de Villèle.[23] In the

---

21 The *Flandre* (Flanders) was a liner of the CGT (*Compagnie générale transatlantique*). It operated on the Central America line 1914-1940 and is not to be confused with the much bigger liner of the same name that was later built for the CGT and put into service in 1954. This latter ship was eventually bought by a Greek cruise company, destroyed by fire in 1994 and scrapped.

22 The *Compagnie générale transatlantique* – also known as the 'French line' – was a shipping company founded in 1861. In 1977 it merged with the *Compagnie des Messageries Maritimes* to form the *Compagnie Générale Maritime*. The latter was privatized in 1996 and merged with the *Compagnie Maritime d'Affrètement* to form the still-trading conglomerate CMA-CGM, the third largest shipping line in the world.

23 Jean-Baptiste de Villèle (1773-1854) served several terms as French prime minister and was one of the Ultra-Royalist leaders during the period known as the Bourbon Restoration. Coincidentally, he had made his political reputation in the Colonies, first in France's Caribbean colonies, but later and more especially in the Indian Ocean colony, Île de Bourbon (the former name of the French *département d'outre-mer*, the island of Réunion), where he defended the distinct interests of the overseas territories.

foreground of these scenes there are huge heaps of coiled rope and, beside them, weeping slaves with woolly hair and prominent jaws.

I'm swallowed up in a single gulp along with my trunk. Soon we're alone together in the square cabin: myself a soft horizontal parcel, my trunk a hard vertical package, the two of us engaged in the most enriching of conversations. Already I can hear the sound of the drawbridge being lowered back onto the pier as this hyphen linking land and water is retracted. The anchors release their affectionate grip, the chain is wound around the capstan and we're off, floating away.

NOVEMBER 12TH

This morning the sea is peaceful and blue. Immediately upon waking, I sense the sun from the heat of the sheet metal and from the shuffling of marbled shapes across my firmly bolted ceiling. Last January, we had to sail forty-eight hours further south to the Azores before the air warmed up. This time, as we emerge from the Bay of Biscay the weather is almost summery.

Lunch is at 11 a.m., but nobody has an appetite. Apart from our ships, only convents and barracks hang on like this to the French meal times of two centuries ago.

There's nothing uglier on this God-given earth than the voices of Spanish women.

The stopovers in Spain are at Santander, Gijón and La Coruña. The transatlantic liners come like leeches to suck up the Basque, Asturian and Galician manpower that they will eventually discharge into the cane-fields. The emigrants arrive out to sea in the middle of the night. Standing dark and gaunt in the tugs with their arms folded across their bellies, they look like depictions of the damned in Early Flemish art. Other boats, loaded with oranges, follow in their wake, lit up like burning embers by candles protected from the wind with cones of oiled paper. Sluggish white gulls emerge from the darkness like etchings and fly across the luminous triangle projected by our navigation lights.

CARIBBEAN WINTER

On deck, Spanish priests walk by like the ghosts depicted in Goyaesque ink-drawings. They are chatting with commercial travellers who seem to have no visible goods to trade and who look just like the priests. This is because they really are priests and are only wearing this commercial disguise in order to gain entry to Mexico.

Small Basque berets crown thirteenth-century skulls. For, just as English and Spanish physiognomies stand out as such, so too do Gothic cheekbones, Renaissance brows, eighteenth-century hairstyles and 1830s noses. It's as though past epochs were different countries.

Children are screaming. They're soothed by the swaying of Indian nannies but are made fretful again by the rocking of the waves. Frenchmen walk up and down taking dainty little steps. They have rounded backs, their hands are plunged deep into their trouser pockets and their spines sit right on top of their pelvis. They will soon be fattened up by the wonderful cooking on board. You can overhear their conversation: 'Now if I were the government...' As my porthole fills with sea and sky alternately, I can hear Colombian girls singing, arm-in-arm like a string of rosary beads. I'm dreaming of the opposite of this harsh Galician landscape carved in icy granite, imagining places to come, lands of sun, pineapples and languor, lying below snow-covered volcanoes with unpronounceable names.

The voyage lasts twelve days without a stopover. It's embroidered with naps devoid of all desire to sleep and by meals devoid of all real hunger. Like a girl in a brothel I'm forever making conquests. I've read just one American newspaper (the equivalent of five issues of the English *Times* and a hundred of the *Petit Parisien*). The shuddering and vibrating of the crankshaft is pounding in my skull. I feel like climbing the masts or polishing the brasses on board: anything to relieve the boredom. A large yacht is visible on the north-south axis. It's heading for Morocco, its sails swollen solid.

Two Negroes from first class are talking together: 'My deah, one hundred tousand francs .... deah friend, two hundred tousand francs...'. Just listen to the talk of the man in the street and nine times out of ten you'll find that he's boasting of buying for one hundred grand and selling for twice that sum, or else he's bragging that he got something for nothing.

I've pinned a big photo of an angora cat on the wall. I cut it out of a newspaper. This cat has such a straight-faced expression, such a steady gaze, that all I have to do is to look at him for the boat to stop rolling.

Above us, heading for Africa, migrating birds are fleeing winter: what magnificent cosmopolitans, luxury-class feathers.

NOVEMBER 13TH

As we approach the Azores the air becomes even warmer. It's twenty degrees and showery. The sea is heavy and leaden though there's no swell. Oh to be able to race through meadows! I will never grow to love the sea. Give me a hovel on land any day rather than a palace on water. I've sometimes spent up to eighty days at sea in one single year, but despite that, I've never managed to catch either sea legs or a sea-faring soul.

I've just been approached by a young Frenchman of Israelite descent. He's twenty and is heading with his father to Central America. Like a lot of young men he speaks fast and indistinctly though he expresses himself with confidence and ease. He's got a brilliant mind, supple and precise, and he has worked as hard at his studies as others train for sports. Indeed his regime includes practising real sport for, like all good German Romantics, he has tramped across Europe on foot, classics in hand. His curiosity has a violent streak, however: he doesn't listen when spoken to but is all a-tremor, so extreme is his need to excel.

He's dripping with neo-classical patriotism and he's hostile to material progress. He's also quite energetic, has an ardent esprit

de corps (he's an alumnus of *Polytechnique*[24]) and finds the ideas of
Maurras and Maritain fascinating[25] Life electrifies him: he revels
in the idea of living it to the full and veers between contempt for,
and solidarity with, his own people. He's still agog with tales of
schoolboy pranks and recounts them wittily, in abridged form, for
he has fully grasped the importance of Proustian 'genteel-ness'
(*gentileza*). He has a curious way of endorsing the traditional
French values of honour, courtliness and loyalty, admiring and
even flaunting them, though in the manner of a businessman: 'It
would be a major mistake to demolish this old castle or turn it
into a factory. Instead of pulling it down we should do it up for
the tourists. This kind of ruin brings in big money!'

NOVEMBER 14ᵀᴴ

Oh the children! Wound up by the sea air, they scream and
stomp about, running, crying and fighting with each other.
The modern steamers do boast nurseries and recreation rooms
but the children refuse to go there to play. In fact, that's where
you must head if you want to get some peace. A Venezuelan
priest, one of those prelates long extinct in Spain, is roasting
Havana cigarettes. They glow like red comets along the length
of the upper decks, burning holes in his soutane. Right now he's
fondling a small girl with the consent of her pious family.

The engines are throbbing out a regular rhythm with the
cadences of a healthy pulse.

---

24 The École Polytechnique is the elite, quasi-military college founded by
    Napoleon Bonaparte to train France's top-tier engineers and scientific/
    technical experts.

25 Charles Maurras (1868-1952) was a thinker and writer who belonged
    to the political movement called 'Action Française', which was Royalist
    in inspiration and, as such, fiercely opposed both to republicanism
    and to parliamentary politics. Jacques Maritain (1882-1973) was
    born a Protestant, but later converted, along with his Jewish wife, to
    Catholicism. He was the prolific author of theological/philosophical
    works in the Thomist tradition.

NOVEMBER 15TH

Curious Customs of the Chinese, by A.N. Smith.[26] There are striking resemblances between the Chinese and ourselves. They have a passion for saving money and the knack of making things last by repairing them indefinitely. They also have a gift for cooking, a sense of mistrust, a centuries-old politeness, an inveterate but passive xenophobia, a conservatism regularly upset by the hurricanes of social upheaval, a lack of public spiritedness and the vitality of those elderly folk who have gone beyond being ill. Does this mean, then, that all ancient civilizations are fundamentally similar?

In striking out towards the south, we're deviating from the route towards Havana and abandoning the North American shoreline, which was said by the first navigators, in the words of their beautiful sixteenth-century language, to be 'roughly hewn'. Just what did those explorers feel on first beholding the shores where they expected to find headless men with an eye in the middle of their chest, or dumb peoples with their mouths sealed, folks who fed themselves through their nostrils with a straw? After all, these men were adventurers who thought only of gold. It was the promise of treasure, and that alone, that brought about the discovery of the modern world.

Solni[27] had regaled them with tales of golden ants with lions' claws and with images of dragons' heads stuffed with precious gems. What an alluring prospect for young Spaniards raised on chickpeas!

---

26 This work must be Arthur Henderson Smith's *Chinese Characteristics* (New York: Revell, 1894). Smith (1845-1932) was an American missionary who spent over fifty years in China and who interpreted that country for the West in much the same way that Lafcadio Hearn interpreted Japan (though over a much shorter period of time).

27 Solni (Gaius Julius Solinus) was a Latin grammarian, author of *De mirabilibus mundi*, who flourished in the third century. He wrote about mythical ant-lions, depicting them in his *Collectrania Rerum Memorabilium* (later called *Polyhistor*) as huge mastiff dogs with talons like those of lions, useful for scooping up gold.

CARIBBEAN WINTER

NOVEMBER 17TH

We've hit some saturnine storms. The sea is boiling, stirred up by a deep submarine seething. The huge lunging breakers resemble the curly-haired waves of Hokusai. Beneath the foam they look transparent, willow grey or bottle green. As they approach the ship's railings they slide beneath the boat and lift it aloft from behind.

NOVEMBER 18TH

We're bobbing about precariously now upon a sea the colour of rhubarb. It looks like mucous stirred about with frothing egg-whites. Warm rain has been deluging down for the past forty-eight hours. So as not to fall off the mattress I've been sleeping with my head wedged between two of the bars on my bed. This morning we were hit by a soft swell so enormous that the ship pitched perilously to one side and in the square frame of the porthole the sky was completely replaced by the sea. The mirrors showed only the ocean as the cabin suddenly darkened and I was faced with a vertical wall of water.

I've finally emerged, soaked, from a dream of drowning. For the past fifty hours the cabin, lined with lemon-wood panelling, has been filled with an ominous creaking and groaning. Why is the interior decoration of boats not entrusted to the inventor of pliable upholstery? Surely ocean liners should be given a rubber and fabric finish! Why are they outfitted by Beaux-Arts architects who've never seen a storm in their lives and who want to set afloat imitations of houses that you'd find on the Île Saint-Louis: mansions decked out with marble and wrought iron and furnished à la Louis XV, a style that, even on dry land, induces seasickness? One such decorator came out with the following priceless line at the launch of a large merchant navy ship: 'Amazing: you'd never guess it's a boat.' The time is long gone when people waxed lyrical about the great ocean liners, the nautical equivalent of locomotives. Ever since Lindbergh's feats, we view these Leviathans with impatience, complaining that they're 'too slow'.

Towards midday, the rain stops. There's a break in the clouds and a breath of cool air. We're at thirty degrees latitude. The sea has fewer wrinkles now and the clouds resemble whipped cream.

Yesterday I heard the crew complaining about having to serve so many black West Indian civil servants being transported gratis. It would appear that the latter are, for some inexplicable reason, afforded the same status as white Metropolitan civil servants. This means that every two years they are entitled to a first-class passage to France for themselves and their family to visit the 'motherland'. They clog up the best liners and are highly demanding, like all those who live at the tax-payer's expense. Their presence on board wards off the custom of the Cubans, Colombians and Venezuelans, who are phobic about being seen as black and who now prefer to sail with the English or Dutch lines.

Tonight brings such a downpour of shooting stars that we could be back in August. Up on the bridge I hear someone saying that these meteors are called Leonids because they emanate from the constellation of Leo. In December it will be the turn of Castor and Pollux to light up the tropical skies with a whole new pyrotechnic display.

NOVEMBER 19TH

The sea is no longer a three-dimensional map. It has gone from resembling a mountainous landscape to looking like a flat horizon drawn in a thick, straight line. Now that it has grown heavy and placid, it reminds me of those wonderful staple sauces featured in cookery books.

The most attractive thing about the Tropics is not the vegetation, which is as overdone as the fake forests painted onto the blinds of delicatessen shop-windows, but rather the skies, especially the colours and shapes of the clouds. Far from, as Baudelaire puts it, looking like 'mobile architecture', the tropical skies resemble blow-ups of microscope slides featuring clouds in the shape of vermicelli, spirals and bacilli.

Our latitude is now thirty degrees north. On dry land the birds are donning their carnival feathers. The Creoles speak in their fatigued accents, which are always stymied by the R sound, like horses refusing to jump an insuperable fence. The pineapples are becoming extremely juicy and the marmosets have stopped coughing.

I once knew a great traveller who was only interested in waterfalls. His collection included the Victoria Falls on the Zambezi; the Niagara Falls; the Iguazu Falls in Argentina[28]; the cascades of Kaieteur in British Guiana; the Tequendama Falls beside Bogotá in Colombia; the great falls of Labrador; the waterfalls on the Orange river; the falls of Yosemite and Yellowstone, and of Gerusoppa[29] in southern India. He was still missing the highest of them all: the Paulo Afonso (at 174 metres) in Brazil.

If the fashion for fictionalized biography continues (and it's impossible, of course, to apply enough face paint to the death's head of the past) and if someone should come to write the biography of Marcel Proust, the emphasis must be on the fundamental drama at the heart of Proust's whole existence. I'm thinking here of the fact that Proust was devoid of illusions and of the way he identified with consummate clarity the time he had left to live and what he had left to say. But I'm also remembering how he was in such a hurry, didn't proof his work any more, never went out, only rarely received visitors, and instead wrote and wrote and wrote, his eyes riveted on the words 'The End'. He pulled it off. He did manage to complete his *magnum opus*

---

28 These falls are located on the border between the Argentinian province of Misiones and the Brazilian province of Paraná.

29 Also called the 'Jog' or 'Joga' Falls.

but he collapsed at the finishing line. He had tried to penetrate the essence of Time in order to compress and annihilate it. And Time retaliated, just like the chemical compound takes revenge on the scientist by blowing him up.

Books should be written in the same way that long-haul airplanes are built: maximum resistance for minimum weight.

I've made a new friend. He's a little English Jew of seven, whose parents – fruit exporters – live in Antigua, an island six hours away from Guadeloupe. We play deck tennis together. He's smart and articulate and, beneath his blond locks, he's already wearing a small Oriental mask.

As for my other friend, the young Frenchman who has tramped across Europe, he doesn't pay attention to things. He's quintessentially abstracted, dwelling somewhere in between pure science and literature. Duhamel[30] is his religion, Giraudoux[31] his recreation. He loves Montherlant's[32] pride and, much to my amusement, observes of Drieu[33] that he's 'making a magnificent career out of despair'. He belongs to that class of young French Jews born during the war, who take up boxing, are led by conviction to enlist in the African regiment and by coyness to make eyes at Catholic Rome.

---

30 Georges Duhamel (1884-1966) served as a doctor in World War I but is best known today as a humanist novelist.

31 Jean Giraudoux (1882-1944) was a French playwright and novelist and also a civil servant who worked for the Ministry of Foreign Affairs. He was a close friend of Paul Morand, having acted as his tutor in 1905 after Morand did badly in his philosophy exam for the *baccalauréat*. His most famous play is *La Guerre de Troie n'aura pas lieu* (The Trojan War Will Not Take Place), which was published in 1935.

32   Henry Millon de Montherlant (1985-1972) was a peripatetic author of essays, novels and plays. In his own time, he was famous less for his misogynistic, proto-aristocratic and reactionary, even collaborationist views, than for openly portraying homosexuality in his writing.

33 Pierre Drieu de la Rochelle (1893-1945) was a prolific and well-connected writer whose reputation suffered from the author's self-destructive deviation from socialism to fascism.

CARIBBEAN WINTER

NOVEMBER 20TH

Flying fish. The ship slows down, inching forward in a gelatinous light that is occasionally broken by a dorsal flash of shark. The walls of my cabin creak like a stove over-filled with fuel. Yesterday, there was a charity evening on board. Some Negroes, who had been wearing coloured paper hats, forgot they hadn't taken them off and were earnestly talking politics: 'The law, my dear, the Justinian Code... productivity, pro rata'. Meanwhile, the children were making a terrible din. Towards the front of the ship, a group of Syrian emigrants were dancing in a tight circle to an interminable tune. They were naked beneath their long shirts, wore towelling turbans on their heads and held their hands crossed on their stomachs. I climbed up onto the upper deck and sat down. In the perfectly still sky, the masthead lights were slowly swaying amongst the stars. Towards three in the morning the Great Bear appeared. A famous sonnet mentions 'new stars' climbing up from the horizon; but behind us, as darkness advances, what a European sees rising are ancient stars.

I've picked up *Le Jardin de Bérénice*[34] once again, having first begun to read it twenty years ago. Its characters are bathed in an air so pure, an atmosphere so dry that they are preserved in a pristine state. It's all so consummately French, so limpid, so arid and so acute, so devoid of kindness and so replete with a wry despair and a brave pessimism, in the vein of Barrès[35], Gide

---

34 *Le Jardin de Bérénice* (*JB*) or 'The Garden of Bérénice' (1891) by Maurice Barrès is the first novel in a first trilogy entitled *Le Roman du moi* ('The Novel of the Self'), which also includes *Le Culte du moi* ('The Cult of the Self', 1897). Barrès' second trilogy, *Le Roman de l'énergie nationale*, or 'The Novel of National Energy', begins with *Les Déracinés* ('The Uprooted', 1897).

35 Barrès (1862-1923) was an anti-parliamentarian, anti-Dreyfusard and hypernationalist writer of romantic sensibility who was close to Charles Maurras (see above, note 25).

and all those Malarians. Of course Aigues-Mortes[36] is no longer a condemned city surrounded, like Mantua, by pestilential swamps. It's now a small but prosperous southern town. And just as Barrès, the great aesthete, reinvented himself as a nationalist, so too the swamps of Petite-Secousse[37] have been turned into vineyards spiked with tall factory chimneys.

The reason I love *Le Jardin de Bérénice* so especially is because it's so very dated, and because it is part of the charm of books like these to capture a moment lost to us forever. As Thibaudet[38] so accurately observed, '*L'Éducation sentimentale*[39] tells the tale of 1848, just as *Le Rouge et le noir*[40] is a chronicle of 1830'.

Sea swallows are pursuing the ship like dogs chasing a motorcar. Tomorrow morning we shall see first La Désirade[41] and then Pointe-à-Pitre will appear port side

Today I transcribed this beautiful excerpt from the sonnet of Saint-Gelais[42], a poem written 'as a preface to the History of the Indies':

---

36 Aigues–Mortes is the name of a town in the South of France, located in marshlands. With its moribund and watery connotations, it provides an apt setting for *JB*.

37 Petite Secousse (meaning 'Slight Seizure' or 'petit mal') is the nickname of the eponymous lesbian protagonist of *JB*.

38 Alfred Thibaudet (1874-1936) was a celebrated literary critic of the interwar years. He is widely regarded as having been consummately of his time in his conservatism and anti-democratic outlook. He was a convinced Europeanist who coined the expression 'Republic of Professors'.

39 *L'Éducation sentimentale* (1869) is a realist *Bildungsroman* by the author of *Madame Bovary* (1856), Gustave Flaubert.

40 *Le Rouge et le noir* (1830) is Stendhal's chef d'oeuvre, also in the realist tradition.

41 Pointe-à-Pitre is the capital of Guadeloupe, one of the Lesser Antilles or Windward Islands of the Caribbean. Since 1946 it has been a *département d'outre-mer* of France, like Martinique and Guyane, but in 1927 it was still a French colony. La Désirade is one of Guadeloupe's principal off-shore islands and it is visible from the capital.

42 Mellin de Saint-Gelais (1491-1558) was King François I's poet laureate and this poem bears the title 'Sonet pour mectre audevant de l'histoire des Indes' (Sonnet – to preface the History of the Indies).

CARIBBEAN WINTER

A different ocean bounded by other shores
And far above these a different sky,
Like the land and sea beneath,
Roved by other kinds of creature.
Happy Columbus who first went in search of them,
And happier still those who conquered them,
Thus uniting one hemisphere with the other.
It's for the Dauphin himself to behold these strange seas;
It's his prerogative to fill with praise
The vast curve of the paternal crescent.

A writer is a medium. His trump card is his vim and if he carries on writing after he has lost that vitality, he'll sound like a worn-out record; he'll be a fraud and will end up being found out. But if he manages to fool his contemporaries right up to the end, the hoax will only be discovered by posterity after he is long dead and gone.

POINTE-À-PITRE

In the morning Guadeloupe lies before our eyes and to the left, Marie-Galante and Dominica. The hilly green landscape could almost be Swiss, were it not for the coconut trees on the beach. It's high season for the flowers and the water is silver, shimmering like mercury. In the distance some Negroes are heading up the hills to cut sugar cane, their white pith helmets emphasizing their blackness. Meanwhile, some Mulatto women dressed in pink stripes have come to flatten their noses against the shop windows of the *Bon Marché*, the ship's novelty goods boutique. Fruit is being hauled on board, some of it very green. There are bananas, coconuts heavy with milk, sugar apples[43] and avocados – or alligator's eggs as they are called in America.

---

43 According to Lise Winer (*Dictionary of the English/Creole of Trinidad & Tobago: on Historical Principles*, Montreal: McGill-Queens University Press) sugar apples ('pommes-cannelles' in French), sometimes called sweetsops, are the heart-shaped fruits of a small tree; they have greenish yellow, bumpy skins and a white, yellow-tinged pulp.

It's raining as I disembark, stepping via a rotting pontoon right into the town's detritus. My face is glistening and my clothes are soaked right through. I'm met by a scene of dilapidation and neglect, of emaciated, hump-backed cattle and ancient American cars. It's quite obvious that all the Negroes here have the vote. They are wearing the stony, hostile and malevolent expressions of people set to nurse their bad humour for another four years. The streets are lined with small huts one storey high and the large patches of greenish damp marking the walls are clear warnings that the rainy season is not over yet.

The most entrancing thing about Pointe-à-Pitre is the big market square. All of a sudden I'm in the midst of three or four hundred Negresses. Some are buying, others are selling. All of them are wearing Madras cotton turbans knotted into two peaks. Their dresses have bright or dark flowers on a background of pink, pistachio, turquoise or light green and all of them have those flounces typical of the tail-end of the eighteenth century. For the Negroes those were the last years of true elegance. They spelt the demise of high society as, from then on, the only French people sent to the Caribbean were civil servants.

The womenfolk are haggling over a couple of cents. It's clear from their hideous vociferation that certain African dialects use the same word for speech as for strife. Having completed their business they close their stalls and leave, their backs long and vertical, their fronts immobile. Only the whites of their eyes slide a little when you pass them. On their heads some bear a saucepan, others a tray laden with crayfish[44] or lettuces, still others a bowl of chilli peppers.

Had I come across the Caribbean after Africa, that is to say, the copy after the original[45], I would have been deeply disappointed.

---

44 'Langoustes' in French, also called 'shiny lobsters' or 'rock lobsters' in English.
45 In a footnote to *Hiver Caraïbe* (1929), Morand (or his editor) explains that 'the present journey precedes the one described in *Paris-Tombouctou*' (1928). The full title of that book was: *A.O.F.: de Paris à Tombouctou*. It was published by Flammarion. (AOF means *Afrique Occidentale Française* or 'French West Africa').

CARIBBEAN WINTER

But as it is, I have come here after having seen the black states of North America and am, on the contrary, enchanted by the colour and the poetry of the Caribbean. The place is impoverished and cash-strapped, certainly. Yet the boisterousness, the clamour, the singing, the vivid colours of the dresses, the primitive customs of the plantations, the hysterical, almost feline, love affairs – facets of life fast disappearing in the United States – can still be found here. And so the *tignon*, that knotted head-dress made of Madras cotton, which is already a thing of the past in New Orleans even though it so becomes the Negresses, is still widely worn here. Indeed, there is more originality in the tiny universe of Pointe-à-Pitre than in the whole of North America put together.

On the other side of the footpath, some Blacks are standing with fighting cocks tucked under their arms. (Cock-fighting too is outlawed in the United States.)

Our stopover is short-lived. We climb slowly on a pot-holed road up through fields of sugar cane scattered with wooden huts on stilts. Their French windows are thrown open and, on the ground beneath the floor, scrawny fowl and some of those black pigs found in the Tropics are grubbing around. The corrugated iron roofs have fake red tiles painted onto them. The soil is crimson and the beauty of the people's dark skin is set off by the luxuriant landscape and by knotted turbans in orange or sulphur-coloured check fabric. Peeping up from the sea of cane and corn, the rough-woven straw hats are reminiscent of the Sudan. The women stop and, arms akimbo, shout cheerful insults in our direction. Beneath the slate-blue mountains, everything is green and chaotic. As we continue to climb, the air turns cooler. To our left, the silver-grey sea stretches out with promontories protruding into it. Through the tufts of the palm trees I spot the Saintes archipelago. There is no beach, for the sand cannot hold back the vegetation. Only the water can arrest its advance. The crossroads are marked by altars and crucifixes, or else by Madonnas made of blue cast-iron. There are also monuments to the war dead, featuring mortally wounded French soldiers sculpted in marble. This is a major blunder, however, because, for the Negroes, the victor is immortal: he is impervious to bullets and never dies. Our one and only stop is made to pour the water from a coconut into the car's radiator. When we return to Basse-Terre[46], the jetty and wharf of the CGT[47] are there to meet us, as well as the old fort of black stone, the cathedral, some black petty officers and a small four-mast boat, all lying in the dark shadows crossed now and then by the rubbery flight of the owls.

NOVEMBER 22ND

We leave Guadeloupe on a pitch-black night. The lacklustre ship's band, backed up on the piano by an excellent Russian refugee, sets us on our way. Beneath the astringent strains of the violin, the capstan can be heard to creak and groan. Not a single fire or lighthouse is in sight as we wend our way between the islands – God knows how, for the Navy couldn't be bothered to provide proper lighting. We've picked up some civil servants bound for Martinique[48]: 'mid-colonials' is the less than respectful name given to them by the ship's personnel.

There is only one black cat on board. Naturally, it dines beneath my chair. At each stopover, this cat disembarks, goes for a walk and then embarks again a few seconds before the ship departs. It's playing a dangerous game, for the Negroes adore cat stew.

---

46 Basse-Terre is the western wing of the two-island butterfly-shape formed by Guadeloupe. It is more mountainous than the flatter eastern wing called Grande-Terre, and the capital, Pointe-à-Pitre, is located on the shore close to where the two wings meet. La Désirade is one of Guadeloupe's many off-shore islands, located to the east, off Grande-Terre.

47 See p. 32, note 22.

48 Martinique is Guadeloupe's sister island, sharing its colonial past and administrative status as a *département d'outre-mer* (overseas county) of France.

CARIBBEAN WINTER

I had vowed to rise early so as to glimpse the volcanic Mont Pelé[49] and the city of Saint-Pierre.[50] But when I opened my eyes it was broad daylight and the ship was already making its way below the protrusions of the old moss-covered fortifications of Fort-de-France.[51] All I could see was a mountain of coal, much higher and much sootier than the one in Peking.[52] It formed a blue-black Alpine peak, a perfect foil for the white colonial garments and headgear, as well as for the blue shirts worn by the Mulattoes and the pink turbans of the women porters carrying coal. The deportment of these Negresses is admirable, especially the way their arms, extended above their heads, elevate their bosoms, and the way their erect torsos and the vertical trench line of their spines push back their shoulders. Their beautiful legs are as sleek as the polished shafts of pillars.[53]

The harder the manual work, the more harmonious the movements. I watch a group of labourers – men who are paid by the day – as they advance, pushing before them a heap of ropes. With their lower backs curved into a hollow, they creep forward taking long tiger-like strides and showing a most unusual suppleness and strength. In contrast, the men who are paid by the month for carrying postbags are much less attractive. And as for the Mulattoes,

49 The Mont Pelé or Montagne Pelée (meaning 'Bald Mount/Mountain') is a volcanic mountain located in Martinique.

50 The Mont Pelé erupted on May 8th 1904, devastating the glittering cultural capital of the island, Saint–Pierre, often described as the Paris of the Caribbean, and killing at least twenty-nine thousand people.

51 Fort-de-France is the administrative and commercial capital of Martinique, although Saint-Pierre was regarded, until its destruction, as the artistic, social and glamour capital of the island.

52 Morand's *Rien que la terre* (1926) is based on the Asian expedition of 1925, when Morand travelled via New York and Vancouver to China (Peking and Shanghai) and Japan, but also Thailand (then called Siam), Ceylon and the Philippines. See pp. 7-8.

53 Lafcadio Hearn (1850-1904) devotes an entire chapter of his 'Martinique Sketches', which form the major part of the volume entitled *Two Years in the French West Indies* (New York, Harper's, 1890), to an encomium to Caribbean women porters ('Les Porteuses'). See also p. 56 and p. 94, note 121.

hired and remunerated by the year, all they are required to bear are leather briefcases bursting with papers but they look hideous.

Water pipes crawl across the ground like boa constrictors and above them large square crates are being lowered down from the sky at the end of a steel rope. The colours of mourning are livened up by some patches of iron that have been painted with red lead pigment.

It's not unknown for the mound of quarried black dust to collapse in an avalanche, burying the women porters. As it is, whenever they raise their overloaded baskets onto their heads, a dark shower of coal dust falls down through the holes in the base of the baskets. This is hard labour, Babylonian-style. The women file into the flanks of the steamer as though entering through the side-door of a temple, bearing their offering of a powder so black that, beside it, their bodies appear light-coloured.

You don't see very young girls or old women doing this work like you do in Shanghai. And there are no men either: just these beautiful creatures. For some reason, they make the sign of the cross when they are handed their tokens – five *sous* per load. First they all move in procession towards the entrance to the hold (a path has been cleared for them by degrees by a man wielding a shovel). Then they wait patiently for five or ten minutes, standing straight and motionless, bearing their thirty kilos on their head. In the past they would have worked to the beat of the tam-tam.

The Empress Joséphine with her train of white marble[54] stands, for her part, protected on all sides by a green fence that is

---

54 The statue of Joséphine de Beauharnais (1763-1814) is located in the centre of Fort-de-France on the esplanade called La Savane. It is no longer secluded in the way that Morand describes here. Born J. de Tascher de la Pagerie either in Martinique or St Lucia (her family owned plantations on both islands), Joséphine was brought up in the 'Big House' of the prosperous Martinican estate 'La Pagerie', a building flattened by a hurricane in 1776. Joséphine's first husband was Alexandre de Beauharnais. It is sometimes said that her second husband, Napoleon Bonaparte, was acting partly in his wife's family's interests when in 1802 he revoked the disestablishment of slavery during the French Revolution. At regular intervals, the head of the statue in Fort-de-France is removed as a protest against her colonial associations and currently (2017) the statue is decapitated.

circled in turn by a second, higher fence formed by the trunks of the palm-trees, the latter looking for all the world like umbrellas blown inside-out by the Caribbean wind.

To get to Saint-Pierre on the other side of the island, I hire a car. Would that nothing at all remained of this city in the wake of its Biblical destruction, but one miserable statue has surfaced. Mounted on eight Greek pillars, it depicts – in ashen pale marble – a woman heaving herself up out of the lava. It was sculpted in memory of the eruption by a student from the *École des Beaux-Arts*.[55]

Legend has it that the disaster happened suddenly. In fact, however, it did nothing of the sort. In his report on the catastrophe of May 8th 1904, Mr Lascroux[56] noted that a first earthquake had taken place on April 19th. This was followed by plumes of smoke from the Mont Pelé on April 23rd, lava from the crater on May 3rd, a rain of molten ash on May 4th and a ninety-metre recession of the tide on May 5th. It is also true that a government-appointed commission published a reassuring report on the 6th. Indeed, according to the special correspondent of a Paris newspaper whose articles were much discussed at the time, elections were due to be held in Martinique on May 11th and so, despite the threat from the volcano, people were kept in town to vote. A survivor, Dr Guérin[57], wrote: 'How could

---

55 Madeleine (de) Jouvray is the name of the sculptor who produced this work, 'Saint-Pierre renaissant de ses cendres'. Like Camille Claudel and Antoine Bourdelle, the artist was a student/associate of Auguste Rodin in Paris. While it is not clear when exactly the sculpture was executed, it appears to have been donated to Martinique and to have arrived there in February 1918 and to have been inaugurated in Place Bertin near the quay in Saint-Pierre. It was eventually moved to the ruins of the Theatre of Saint-Pierre where many tourists mistake it for a statue that survived the earthquake. Its centenary was celebrated on May 8th 2017.

56 H. Lascroux, *La Martinique avant et après le désastre de 1902*, Moulins (Allier): 1902 (2nd edition Paris: Hachette/BNF, 2013).

57 These words, attributed to the Martinican distillery owner, Auguste Guérin, who had a narrow escape in 1902, are quoted by Jean Hess in his book, *La Catastrophe de la Martinique: notes d'un reporter*, Paris: Charpentier et Fasquelle, 1902.

people live in a city where, on May 6th, there were almost five centimetres of ash in the streets? It happened because of the elections, no doubt. Three hours after my factory had been swept away, people were posting electioneering posters on the walls.' And so it was that the imperative of universal suffrage took precedence over death itself.

Forty thousand people perished in a rain of fire and rock. It took the lava just three minutes to travel the eight kilometres separating mountain and shore. The red darkness was full of poisonous gases and explosions. And at sea ships disappeared or, with their masts gone, were reduced to phantoms, their decks covered in ash, their sails burned to a cinder. Today the essentials have all been rebuilt. By that I mean the rum factories and the docks where the sugar cane is handled. Outside the town though, nature has taken over; and so the earth has vanquished the fire that rained down from the sky. Sugar plantations now cover the land that slopes down to the sea. As for the Mont Pelé itself, that big earthen abscess with its muddy pus is hidden in the mist. So I never actually saw it, just as I never actually beheld Fukushima.

Saint-Léger Léger[58], who was born on an island close to Guadeloupe, part of his family's fiefdom, once told me that his grandmother[59], from old Creole stock, often mentioned the

---

58 Morand is name-dropping here. It was, no doubt, on the Quai d'Orsay, at the French Ministry of Foreign Affairs, that Morand met Alexis Léger (1887-1975). The young poet/diplomat liked to call himself 'Saint-Leger Leger' (without accents), the pseudonym with which he signed his early poetry. He later forsook that penname for the more mysterious 'Saint-John Perse', under which he was awarded the Nobel Prize for Literature in 1960. The poet seems to have invented the story of his off-shore nativity, since there is no evidence to suggest that he was not in fact born on the Guadeloupean mainland, in Pointe-à-Pitre. See Mary Gallagher, *La Créolité de Saint-John Perse*, Paris: Gallimard, 1998.

59 The D'Ormoy branch of the poet's family belonged to the Guadeloupean plantocracy. The memoirs of the poet's grandmother were published along with those of Elodie Jourdain, a family friend from Martinique who was taken in by the poet's family when the volcano erupted, in *Mémoires de Békées*, ed. Henriette Levillain, Paris: L'Harmattan, 2002.

Martinican catastrophe 'in which seven thousand souls perished. When people objected that the victim toll had been forty thousand, she would reply 'Well yes, if you count the coloured folk!'[60]

Some Negroes are digging around in the earth with their hands; you wouldn't say that they are cultivating the soil as much as sifting it.

Just picture the man who rises when all of nature is already awake and who finds, ready and waiting for him, a steaming cup of coffee and, on his doorstep, his daily newspaper and cheap transport. He has two square meals each day, goes fishing on Sundays and to the cinema on Saturday evenings. He has benefited from free education and is insured and protected against old age and sickness. This is the white worker, the western employee. If we add a small garden and some wine with each meal, then we have the perfect picture of the French labourer.

And now imagine a man who is more or less naked, dressed in rags, and who only has a bowl of rice or a couple of roasted crickets to eat each day. For him the lowliest labour is a godsend. He toils between fifteen and eighteen hours a day, owns nothing and his only pleasure is to have a full stomach from time to time. He sleeps where he can, in the street or in the hold of a ship. Forced to do the hardest work conceivable in countries where there are no machines and where conditions of hygiene can be horrific, this skeletal being is abandoned to his fate. He is protected by no laws, hounded by moneylenders, press-ganged by armies and generally held to ransom. This is the lot of the black labourer and, more generally, of the coloured proletarian.

Clearly, instead of calling both men 'workers', we should find new names for such dissimilar destinies. In the meantime, there is no doubt that, in comparison with coloured people, Whites

---

60 In the biography that he himself composed for the Pléiade edition of his complete works, the poet does mention in these terms his family's reaction to news of the eruption. Saint-John Perse, *Œuvres complètes*, Paris: Gallimard, 1972, p. xii.

– and here I mean all Whites including the poorest of them – constitute a privileged elite.

'The poor', as Chamfort[61] once said – in a statement as true today as it was when he made it – 'are the Negroes of Europe'. But how are we then to regard the real Negroes? Everyone is always someone else's Negro and this fact was always perfectly clear to the Muscovites. 'We should unite the Negroes and the poor,' they argue, 'supplementing the struggle for class equality with a struggle for racial equality.'

Today, this kind of radical dogma is espoused by certain members of the 'aristocracy of whiteness' in the same spirit as the 1789 Revolution was embraced by the intellectual nobility of the eighteenth-century Enlightenment. When we hear public servants with a securely guaranteed future – workers in the armaments industry or primary-school teachers, for example – proclaim themselves Communists, inevitably we think of Lafayette or Mirabeau[62] and all those other fine liberal minds who paid with their heads for their avant-garde snobbery. Although there are two and a half centuries between them, both elites have ended up in the same situation. In one of the greatest mistakes of history, France, a land of forty million people, a land that owes not only all its glory, but its entire *raison d'être*, to luxury or even just to quality, is failing to grasp the fact that it will lose everything if it seeks to measure itself against the rest of the world in a domain so alien to it, that of quantity, where its defeat is guaranteed.

---

61   The one-time courtier-turned revolutionary Sébastien-Roch Nicolas (known as Chamfort) (1741-1794) was a noted author of epigrams and aphorisms.

62   Gilbert du Motier, Marquis de Lafayette (1757-1834) fought as a young man in the American Revolution and was, paradoxically, both a Royalist and Revolutionary throughout and following the late eighteenth-century French Revolution. He lived to take part in the 1830 Revolution in France also. Similarly, Honoré Gabriel Riqueti, Count of Mirabeau (1749-1791), also participated in the French Revolution as a moderate who was favourable to a constitutional monarchy. He died of natural causes in 1791, before his political motivation and position could be conclusively determined.

Having failed to take the measure of the universe other than through books, many Communists imagine that, after the Great Twilight, they will be free to organize France as they wish and to turn it into another Russia: a small Russia, certainly, but a Russia of their very own. They cannot see that, from the very instant that they are incorporated into the ranks of an International World Order, they'll be swallowed up. What they should do instead is learn to read the map of the real world, taking good note of the experience of Africa, India and China. The pedestals of these three monstrously massive continents are being pulverized by Bolshevism. They will inevitably collapse on top of the Communists, burying them beneath their own rubble.

Although they possess the gift of consciousness, Communists invoke the unconscious. Although they have been blessed with intelligence, they court matter, and throw open to the masses the doors of their palaces. For France, as everyone knows, is, in itself, a palace. In comparison with the earth's many frozen or torrid deserts, its dried-up torrents or savage climates, and in comparison with those overpopulated continents where the real proletarian armies are being raised, can our radical Left really be so naive as to think that they will be left to live in peace in their fat Normandy lands, beside their rivers teaming with fish, beneath their clement southern sun (just think of all those merchants made millionaires by the wine derived from the red-earthed Var[63])? Can they really credit that they'll be left to their own devices in this land with its population of barely seventy-eight inhabitants per square kilometre? Do our home-grown French Communists not see what ferocious, implacable brethren they are going to give us?

Where on earth is the police force that could stop the forced entry of millions of Blacks into a country whose borders have disappeared? Which trade union law could outlaw steamers

---

63 The Var river rises in the Alps and flows through Provence, giving its name to a region and *département* in south-eastern France.

packed with Chinese market gardeners coming to cultivate every plot of the French Riviera, to suck up its juice and to impoverish its soil with their antlike labour that knows neither night or day? Which barrier could keep out the Japanese farmers who will come to feed ten mouths with just one of the lunches of one of our Bolshevik taxi-drivers? France will then be to Siberia what a tiny republic of the Italian peninsula might have been to the great French Republic under the *Directoire*.[64] Scarcely will power have been snatched from our bourgeois hands by the peasant and soldier committees of Communism, than these 'nouveau riche' proletarians will find their gates being battered in turn by the waves of Asian-scale migration washing up onto our shores the real poor: that is the dreadful, starving, all-too-real paupers and beggars of Africa and the Caribbean. Our socialist land will then be set upon by those for whom Communism is not just a word or a fashion but an eternal organic state: we will be facing vast hordes reduced to bare hands and teeth, to the outstretched arms and gaping jaws of starvation.

We are driving back down through the island past fountains of bamboo, cascading waterfalls, cool mists hanging low over the mountain summits and various species of trees. The black driver takes the turns on two wheels. (I wouldn't like to be the rear seat of a car being driven by a black driver, or the gearbox of a car in the hands of a Chinese chauffeur). Our own pilot makes as much noise as possible, honking his horn and aiming the car straight at the nobodies who are, in fact, his own kith and kin.

What a paradise the Americans would set up for themselves here...

'Tomorrow we'll be in Trinidad!' says the barman. 'And it's quite something. It's so obvious that the English are the ones in charge there!' He's interrupted in these unpatriotic remarks by some of the expats who are swarming all over the boat

---

64 The post-revolutionary French regime known as the *Directoire* (1795-99) produced a time of intense military expansionism (particularly into Italy and Egypt).

and calling for 'A bottle of Moët and six champagne glasses!' Some Negresses are arguing on the bridge as they set up their hammocks for the night.

A native arrives at my cabin door with a telegram. 'It hasn't been paid for,' he announces with considerable self-assurance. I retort that in France it's not customary to send a telegram without payment upfront. 'Oh alright then,' he replies, giving in.

Ah, the cast-iron kiosk[65] of the Rue de la Liberté! Ah, the statue of Schoelcher[66], Liberator of the Blacks! As for the beautiful Martinican countryside, I feel that I'm seeing it for the second time, so vivid are the memories inspired by Lafcadio Hearn's *Two Years in the French [West] Indies*[67], a book full of sensuality and joie de vivre, its pages perfumed by the scent of the Negresses. Hearn's passion for coloured women is the key to that entire book.

The opaque and controversial question of racial mixture requires close and careful study. It's even more critically important in the contemporary context, given that what used to be the exception is now set to become the rule. The development of communications inevitably means that miscegenation will become ever more widespread. Before the war the number of

---

65 These press kiosks belong to the 'belle époque' style of French street furniture that is made of elegant wrought-iron and usually painted bottle green like the Métro entrance canopies and the equally distinctive 'colonnes Morris' that serve as advertising pillars.

66 Victor Schoelcher (1804-1893), a writer and philanthropist, is credited with having engineered the ratification in France in April 1848 of the *Decree of the Abolition of Slavery* (for, following its abolition during the French Revolution, Bonaparte had re-established slavery in the French Caribbean in 1802). Born in Paris to an industrialist father from Alsace, Schoelcher first encountered slavery in Cuba when he was sent there to further the family business. He is multiply commemorated in Martinique and in Guadeloupe.

67 Lafcadio Hearn (1850-1904), a Greco-Irish-American writer, was commissioned in 1887 by *Harper's Magazine* to travel throughout the Caribbean basin. His articles on his travels there and on his subsequent prolonged stay on the island of Martinique were subsequently collected and published by Harper's in 1890 under the title quoted by Morand. See above, p. 48, note 53.

crossbreeds was estimated at eighteen million out of a total world population of 1.2 billion people, but this proportion must have doubled by now.

It is in the US and in Germany that the matter of racial mixture, directly related to theories of eugenics, has been most closely studied. In France, nobody since Broca[68] has studied the question in the round. In 1908, the Paris Society of Anthropology set up a standing commission to study ethnic mixing. Opening the proceedings, the commission's chairman, Dr Papillot, a liberal and a moderate, positioned himself midway between the two sides of the debate: 'We are facing a problem of exceptional gravity and one that has, up to now, always been approached through theoretical deduction. Some thinkers, invoking a religion-tinged humanitarianism, advocate the fusion of all the different races. Others, in the name of aristocratic principles that have never been fully respected, demand the absolute exclusion of the inferior races. The former ignore the imperative of natural selection, without which we would all still be anthropoids; the latter forget that even the most exclusive of aristocracies are renewed by crossings...'.

The arguments of the second side (ie. Gobineau[69] and the Germano-American partisans of Aryanism) still make an impression on me in so far as they point out that interbreeding is not productive, since it never results in a specific stable race. That is, cross-breeding cannot create a new or original type with a stable identity (for, as Mendel[70] found, the return to the pure

68 In 1859, Pierre Paul Broca (1824-1880), a medical scientist and craniologist, founded the Anthropological Society of Paris.

69 Joseph Arthur, Comte de Gobineau (1816-1882) was a diplomat/ traveller and the author of a five-volume work about racial inequality (*Essai sur l'inégalité des races humaines*) which appeared between 1853 and 1855. He was a notorious proponent of so-called 'scientific racism', of the dangers of racial mixing and of the superiority of the 'white race'.

70 Gregor Mendel (1822-1884), an Augustinian monk living in what is today the Czech Republic, founded genetics by establishing the basic rules of heredity. He confirmed that cross-breeding could favour the transmission of desirable traits.

type is one of the laws of mixed heredity). Instead, it engenders hybrids that die out in the third generation. Indeed, if, as Emerson says, nature loves mixture, it does not approve of all mixes. Visit any black American university or college and you will see the throngs of ever so serious, ever so studious half-castes, whose refined European features have gone missing beneath dreadful heads of woolly hair. You'll also see blond or red-haired Negresses, not to mention all those souls consumed by contradictory desires and all those bodies whose proportions have been violated by the struggle between two inheritances. These spectacles cannot but inspire the anguished pity mixed with repulsion aroused by all human anomalies. In that sense, the beautiful Negresses of the Sudan, who feel no physical attraction for the European male, are following a very sensible instinct: namely, respect for racial purity. Humanity as a whole is apparently governed by two fundamental laws of sexual gravitation: racially speaking, men want to diversify willy-nilly, whereas women prefer to maintain racial selection and to protect racial integrity.

The USA does not allow people of colour to enter its territory, although this defensive initiative, a historical first, will not perhaps become the rule everywhere. It seems likely to me that the day will come when, as a result of wars and migrations and under the pressure of invasions, peaceful or otherwise, the races of the universe will blend into one single variety, even if this unified race might become susceptible again afterwards to differentiation.

NOVEMBER 23ʳᵈ

This is a morning of leaden skies and molten heat. All things appear in various shades of grey, veering between white and black, like in the cinema. The hysterical sea is moved by a low, raging swell. Towards one o'clock in the afternoon we're within sight of a necklace of mountainous islands, each clad in a hairy coat of green fur. The largest one is Trinidad. We pass between two of these islands, advancing right to the very back of a great bay before dropping anchor in front of Port of Spain. There we are loaded aboard an old petrol-powered dinghy driven by a worthy Negro, bristling with authority. He terrorizes the other Negroes who lack his stripes and must make do instead with makeshift insignia. One of these is sporting an enamel badge inscribed with the name 'Dunlop'. Another has the English word 'Ice' embroidered in gold on his uniform. I saw not a single Englishman during the entire stopover. Only Blacks and Hindoos. At the front of our dinghy a hunting horn is attached to the ceiling by a piece of string. The decorated Negro is blowing it, producing a comical congested sound reminiscent of the hunting horns of Bayreuth[71] used to summon back from the forest those tourists who had escaped during the interval...

Port of Spain looks like Vancouver, Ceylon or Hong Kong. It resembles all the English colonies, which in turn mimic England, more precisely its surfaced roads, its shops that close at four in the afternoon, its parkland, tennis courts, bungalows, bibles and zoos. And, of course, its Hindoo coolies.[72] Braving the torrential daily downpour we take the so-called Saddle Trail into the mountains via splendid highways, all the more splendidly surfaced since the island contains one of the two biggest asphalt lakes in the world.

The sun does nothing for these landscapes, which need to be seen in the rain, when woolly clouds envelope the summits and when the soaked bamboos and the waterfalls mean that the very air in the atmosphere entirely gives way to water.

---

71 The inaugural Richard Wagner music festival was held in Bayreuth (located in Bavaria) in 1876 and is still running annually.

72 The term 'Coolie' (derived from a Hindi word meaning 'porter') referred originally in the Caribbean to indentured workers from the subcontinent of India, drafted in throughout the nineteenth century to replace slave labour. It later came to mean labourers of variable Asian origin (principally Indian or Chinese) and could also be used pejoratively as a racist slur.

CARIBBEAN WINTER

All of a sudden I'm struck by the extreme monotony of the Tropics. There are hardly any birds and the cattle are scrawny and miserable. There are no cats, the dogs are starving and there are only four or five species of flower, always the same ones. People are wont to extoll the luxuriant imagination of nature in the Tropics, but what is it compared with the fertile inventiveness of even the most insignificant Dutch horticulturalist who creates a hundred new varieties for every flower-show? The rose and the carnation, we are told, came from Persia and Asia. But they are so simple! Whereas the thin red tulips on the ceramics of Rhodes have only bloomed in Haarlem!

The ship's passengers have banded together to form one of those sarcastic and cynical, noisy and anarchical groups known as a fraternity of Frenchmen. At a very British tea-party we shock the protestant Negresses by laughing on a Sunday, eating our sandwiches without a fork and by taking a snack at an hour when we should by rights be having dinner. Why is it that, as soon as we find ourselves in England or in an English colony, we feel this irresistible need to give scandal, not to sing the hymns, not to register with the police and to dunk our bread into our hot chocolate?

We are back on board at nine o'clock, accompanied by a number of the unhappy inhabitants of Port of Spain. For these would-be night owls, who are condemned to an early bedtime each evening, the only nightlife on offer is the prospect of downing a bottle of champagne once a fortnight on board the floating cabarets that are the French boats. To think that these steamers that bore us passengers to tears hold such a strong attraction for certain landlubbers!

Trinidad was so baptized by Columbus, who made a habit of eradicating the beautiful though primitive Indian names, replacing them with ponderous Catholic labels. Prior to him, the island had been known as the 'Land of the Humming Bird'.

Trinidad is the best strategic position in the Caribbean for surveillance of the route from North to South America.

NOVEMBER 24TH

After a suffocating night, we awaken this morning on the Venezuelan coast, at Carúpano. Nobody disembarks and the only person who comes on board is the Venezuelan governor, who is in search of toothpicks. This fellow is a hedonist: French toothpicks, being made of feathers, are wonderfully flexible and solid, yet they are unknown throughout the rest of the world. The only ones widely available are those horrid Japanese splinters that lacerate the gums and get stuck between the teeth.

The bay of Carúpano is bristling with pelicans. At rest with folded wings these birds are scarcely bigger than a duck. However, as soon as they take off, beating the air with the great curves of their angular wings and thrusting out their beaks – shaped like the blade of a scythe – they show all their Baudelairean grandeur. In a flash they swoop down on the fish and spear them, never missing their target.

The people here have pottery-coloured skin, the same shade as the skin of certain Japanese fishermen. They approach us in boats made of hollowed-out tree trunks and are well used to coming out to swap their fish for our fresh bread. They give us *bonitos*, a sort of metre-long mackerel, as well as flat fish with sickle-shaped fins and skin with yellow highlights, the colour of sulphur. The jellyfish floating on the water between two tides look like the noodles suspended in Italian soup.

We shall be sailing along the Venezuelan coast now for wenty-four hours.

- Here, nobody ever drowns, claims the Captain.
- Really?
- No, the sharks would get to them first.

NOVEMBER 25TH

The following morning, we were heading into La Guaira, Venezuela's chief port, which completely encircled us. It was like making for a giant painted panel. The mountains, towering fifteen hundred metres above the port, are layered and laminated, incised with volcanic ridges. Torrents of greenery tumble into the ravines and the trees, manhandled by the sea winds, are hanging onto rocks tinted the dreadful shade of red that one associates with kosher butchers in the ghettos. The slopes are covered in long low houses, brightly painted in washing-powder blue, pink and green. Further down lie the docks, visible between the coconut trees. And further down still are the Caribbean schooners and brigs, all painted bathtub white. It's atrociously hot. As soon as we can, we disembark and, in a flash, hundreds of cars appear, all offering to bring us up to Caracas, the capital city of Venezuela. Just like children, young countries adore noise. To wow the pedestrians and intimidate their colleagues, the native drivers honk their horns continuously, turning the streets into one long roar.

The road that takes us a thousand metres higher up, as far as Caracas, is a masterpiece of engineering. Its technical perfection points to this being the work of a star pupil from *Ponts et Chaussées*.[73] And it was in actual fact designed by a Frenchman. The gradients, the calculation of the slopes, the proportions of the curves, all point to a virtuoso of triangulation. This one really let himself go, making things as arduous as possible for himself, all the better to surmount the difficulties triumphantly, just like in the story of the dictation that Mérimée set for Napoleon III.[74] We are climbing corkscrew-fashion, rising first above a leper colony whose pink roof seems to have been itself contaminated by the disease, and then right up into the clouds that all too soon

---

73 Literally 'Bridges and Highways', this is the most prestigious of French colleges of Civil Engineering; it was established in Paris in 1744.

74 The writer Prosper Mérimée (1803-1870), author of *Carmen*, was commissioned by the Empress Eugénie to compose a dictation exercise for the court of Napoléon III. The Emperor himself is said to have made seventy-five mistakes, the Empress seventy-two, Alexandre Dumas (Jr) twenty-four and the Austrian ambassador, Metternich, just three!

hide the summits from view. Here we're on the same level as the sky, while down below us everything is tumbling into the sea. The air is starting to cool down and the Negroes of the lower coastline have given way to Indians. On this luxurious highway that twists its contorted way around the mountain, the cars travel bumper to bumper, intimidating one another in their efforts to overtake. They take bends on the wing, almost plunging into the void and paying no heed at all to the sign *ALERTA* engraved on the base of an equestrian statue. Above the notice – right where the horse used to be – stands an old car that has been fished out of the ravine and displayed as a warning. As soon as a car somersaults off the road, it's rapidly relieved of all of its most desirable accessories so that it soon looks like one of those corpses devoured by vultures (or *zopilotes*[75]). The latter are the only waste disposal agents at work in Caracas. Even though the entire highway is surfaced with concrete, nature has still done its worst to this work of art. Everywhere lies evidence of landslides and subsidence and it's left to the guests of President Gómez' prisons to clear away the crushed remains of boulders. Sometimes when a mudslide takes place beneath the road, it leaves the highway intact, so that its cement crust appears to hang in mid-air above the void.

We are arriving now in the Caracas suburbs. Unlike Mexico and Lima, the Venezuelan capital boasts no ancient colonial-style houses. Venezuela was always regarded as a rather poor colony by the Spaniards and they spent very little on it. Certainly, it could boast neither the silver of Mexico, the gold of Peru, nor the emeralds of Colombia, although the Venezuelan oilfields of Maracaibo are a recent source of wealth. I must admit, however, to liking its modern Indian idiom, spare as it is, and somewhat uncivilized and utilitarian. I like the cubes of rough masonry, the loud colours, the simple street grids and this suburban style where

---

75 *Zopilotes* or black vultures were still common as street scavengers in Mexico as late as the second decade of the twentieth century.

the screaming untidiness of cinema posters forms the backdrop to a new and original civilization. I'm told that miscegenation is the order of the day in Venezuela. Even the animals form combinations not previously known in nature. The dogs look like hippogriffs, the horses like donkeys, the donkeys like fish and the fish like panthers. As for Venezuelan society, it's divided into an infinite number of clans, each claiming a better bloodline than the next. At sixteen or seventeen, Venezuelan girls are irresistible. Like Spanish girls, they wear lots of make-up and, with their cherry lips, Indian cheekbones, Inca eyes, copper-coloured skin and their scarves and clothes of light, see-through chiffon, they are the jewels in the crown of this otherwise staid land. The Syrians make a fortune by selling them silk. Arriving from the Middle East by the village load, these immigrants work first as door-to-door salesmen, then buy a shop and, ten years later, leave as millionaires. Just like in Dakar or Mexico, and indeed everywhere else after the war, their rapaciousness soon gets the better of the local businessmen.

The French consulates are overrun by Syrians. In fact, the citizens of this one French protectorate[76] make more work for our diplomatic corps than a whole colony put together. They demand our help at all hours of the day or night without showing the least gratitude, without paying the slightest tax and often without speaking a single word of French.

Venezuelans are, in general, Francophiles. Every wealthy Venezuelan family has a *pied-à-terre* in Paris and goes shopping there each year. For them, France presents none of the disadvantages of the United States. With its genial outward appearance of pleasure-seeking and luxury, it's perceived as unthreatening.

---

76 Morand is technically mistaken in calling Syria a French 'protectorate'. In fact, the status of France's relation to both Syria and the Lebanon was that of a *mandat* or mandate, under the League of Nations agreement that established it after World War I. This was a more provisional and looser kind of tutelage than that of a 'protectorate' like Tunisia (though of course the status of 'protectorate' was in turn associated with a less complete form of control than that imposed on a 'colony').

One man alone dominates the Venezuelan past, namely Bolívar. His story has been most readably recounted by M. Vaucaire[77], even if this version does display an implicit ingratitude towards the previous biographer, my deceased colleague in Foreign Affairs, Mr Mancini.[78] Indeed, Bolívar is such a hero that his bronze statue stands on the Hippodrome (Racecourse) promenade (if such a name can be accurately bestowed on a meadow where the only races held nowadays are dog-races).

Similarly, one man alone, President Gómez, towers over the Venezuelan present. Gómez is an astonishing specimen of the South American dictator class. He's a benevolent Indian tyrant, an illiterate catapulted into the rank of General on a whim of the former president, one General Castro, whom Gómez subsequently deposed without a second thought[79]. Gómez looks after his own business interests no less than after those of the state. He's immensely wealthy and has countless numbers of illegitimate offspring. Just like one of the Biblical patriarchs, whose seed yielded a thousand generations, he's widely believed to have fathered seventy-five children. His eldest son holds the monopoly on pearl fishing in Santa Margarita while Gómez himself holds the national herd in trust. He owns a *hacienda* of two hundred

---

77 Jules Vaucaire, *Bolívar, El Libertador: la vivante histoire*, Paris: Grasset, 1928. The earlier study by Mancini is *L'Émancipation des colonies espagnoles des origines à nos jours*, Paris: Perrin et Compagnie, 1912.

78 Simón Bolívar (1783-1830) was a Venezuelan military and political leader. He was known as *El Libertador* because of the role he played in the anti-imperial struggle against Spanish power and in the establishment of Venezuela.

79 Of almost entirely Indian descent and an autodidact, Juan Vicente Gómez (1857-1935) joined the private army of the dissident Cipriano Castro in 1899. When Castro's paramilitaries defeated the government forces, took Caracas and deposed the president, Castro appointed Gómez as his vice-president. However Gómez later deposed Castro and took over as president in 1908; he was a dictator but is held to have been successful in his management of the Venezuelan economy, particularly the oil economy.

thousand hectares, where soldiers of the Venezuelan army spend their entire military service learning about farm-work in an arrangement that seems of considerable benefit to all concerned. His wealth is estimated at one and a quarter billion francs, not counting the balances on his foreign bank accounts. Gómez never leaves Venezuela, because history shows that he would no sooner reach Trinidad than he would be toppled by a revolution. On any given occasion nobody knows where the president is sleeping or in which car he is travelling. According to some Venezuelans who have sought refuge in Europe, he tortures his victims by hanging them from their testicles. He's a stiff little man with a big moustache, squeezed into his buttoned-up shirt collar. He has indefatigable energy, pays his doctors in gold, is kept alive by injections and fears death. He knows nothing about Europe, ignores all diplomatic objections and tells all the ambassadors appointed to his country: 'If you're not happy, you can get on a boat and leave.'

Afternoon dance parties are the most favoured form of hospitality in Caracas. The following warning is displayed, I'm told, on a poster: 'No dancing with the same partner twice.' Venezuelan vendettas are famously fierce, especially if the champagne has been flowing freely. In the embassies, if enough drink is not served, the guests tackle the host directly, tapping him on the back: 'Come now, Your Excellency, where are you hiding the Pommery?'[80]

This evening, following our rapid and quite terrifying descent by car from Caracas in the rain and the dark, we are to set sail for Curaçao.

NOVEMBER 26TH

Towards 5 p.m. we're standing like a herd of cattle gathered at noon beneath the only tree on the prairie. Huddled under the

---

80 A brand of champagne from the Elizabethan-style estate founded in the nineteenth century in the Champagne region of France by a Madame Pommery.

canvas hood at the rear of the boat and surrounded by a fiery sea, we catch sight of the small Dutch island of Curaçao. In profile, with its crenellated relief, it resembles the cross-section of a rock deposited upon the sea. Suspended right above it for a few minutes is the most beautiful pink cloud that I've ever seen; it definitely deserves a much more alluring name than 'cumulus'. As we approach, we can make out on the coastline a row of brightly coloured little houses. What a surprise: we're pulling in to Holland! Amid the facades adorned with steps, swirls and tiled roofs, all that's missing are the brass bands, the polders and the cows. And now we're met by yet another surprise: we are coming right into the very heart of the town via an immense canal. Along it are moored brigs, schooners, cargo ships, tankers and steamboats. Right inside this unusual island, the canal opens up into a circular harbour, a water-filled basin that would easily hold several navy fleets. How did the English let all this slip through their fingers? There's a suffocating smell of oil. In fact, all the Royal Dutch-owned oil that's drilled in Maracaibo (just across from Curaçao) is brought here to be refined; this explains the rows of reservoirs lined up along the coast.

One of my Parisian friends sent me the following delicious note on Curaçao. 'Curaçao is a Dutch colony but no one there speaks Dutch. A hundred years ago, the Dutch got all uppity and banished lots of Jews who went off and settled in Chile and Peru. Little by little, however, they came back to Curaçao where they were met by a version of Holland.

'Like all Dutch possessions, Curaçao is a major smuggling hub because it's a free port. The entire Dutch colony is Jewish and all the Jews are related to one another. I'm giving you a letter of introduction to Mr Samuel, one of our main clients. The only decent hotel is the *Americano*, on the quay. From your windows you'll have a good view of the steamboat that will come from Dutch Guiana and bring you to Haiti. Don't forget that it's pointless to try to get a room with a bathroom en suite because there's no water in Curaçao. It's all brought in from South America so that a single bath costs two hundred gold cents. The people of Curaçao speak an incomprehensible language called Papiamento, a mixture of Yiddish, Spanish and Dutch.'

All along the central canal lies a row of ancient forts, more fearsome than functional. Behind them is the governor's palace, in First Empire style, yellow with white stuccowork. Then come houses that look just like those of Leiden or Amsterdam. Since they accommodate the various consulates, they are flying the flags of every country in the world. Every language is spoken on the island, all currencies are accepted and all kinds of adventurers are there to be consorted with. It's a sort of prefiguration of the future of humanity, where people will no longer be yellow, white, or negro, but universally mixed and all busy selling things to one another.

Curaçao is the largest port in the whole Caribbean and has an amazing turnover of boats. The swing bridge is in motion round the clock, pivoting to admit cargo ships, oil tankers and – in the winter – American yachts. In the cafés there are quite a few Frenchmen who have escaped from French Guiana.[81]

The hotel is a wooden building. It has been painted and repainted with those wonderful boat varnishes – green, blue or white – that that the Dutch use on their houses. Its walls are adorned with landscape paintings incrusted with mother-of-pearl. The picture frames are painted the same colour as the walls and I find this transition between picture and wall most effective as a design idea. The fare is very Dutch: soup for lunch, warm ham for breakfast and every meal is accompanied by jugs of beer, raw cabbage salad, orange marmalade and whiskey.

NOVEMBER 27TH

This morning, at dawn, a Dutch cruise ship turns up on the calm river, passing in front of little houses framed in green by the

---

81 We can presume that Morand is referring here to fugitives from the notorious French penal colony or *bagne*, located in French Guiana.

rising sun. With great solemnity, it gives a reedy rendering of the national anthem, obliging the governor to make an appearance on his balcony to raise the flag. It then slides down the river, well pleased with its assembled crew dressed in white and bearing arms.

NOVEMBER 28TH

My own ship doesn't leave until this evening so I'm going to see an ostrich farm. The interior of the island is the most desert-like place one could possibly imagine. No coconut or banana trees, just naked rock clothed only in stunted plants like cactus candelabras or thorny dwarf palms. The landscape winces like a human face. Not one of the nice new cars that roar up and down the single surfaced thoroughfare in the town would risk venturing beyond the town walls, where the trail has been washed away by the rain. Small falcons, perched on the cactus plants, lie in wait for the shy little birds that fly low and hop around like partridges.

The ostrich farm is pitiful. Fifty bald birds reveal their scrawny and indecently nude thighs. 'The thighs of the ostrich,' writes Labat[82], 'are a dirty white with reddish tinges, making them look just like human faces.' 'Did nature decide,' he goes on to wonder, 'that it was useless to clothe in feather padding a head that had no brain to lose? These feathers are the ostrich's

---

82 Jean-Baptiste Labat (1663-1738) landed in Martinique in 1694. A Dominican missionary, usually called Le Père Labat (Father Labat), he had a career that combined the activities of an explorer, a colonialist, a slave-holding entrepreneur and a man of science (engineering and botany especially), whose chief laboratory was Martinique's slavery-based sugar industry. His two major works, written up in Paris after he returned to Europe in 1706, were the six-volume work *Nouveau voyage aux îles de l'Amérique* (New Voyage to the American Isles) which appeared in Paris in 1722. He also wrote on West Africa and on Ethiopia, basing his text on notes taken by other missionaries. This is the case of *Voyage du Chevalier Demarchais en Guinée, aux îles voisines, et à Cayenne, fait en 1725, 1726, et 1727*, which appeared in 1730.

best feature, ever since luxury designers started to use them to decorate helmets, garters, Janissary headgear[83], theatre costumes, pedestals, the pillars of four-poster beds, and even churches.'

If you were to offer a ring to an ostrich – apparently they are particularly partial to diamonds (perhaps a throwback to South Africa which is their native land, after all) – it will attempt to swallow it. Would you then have to buy the bird and carry it off, complete with the ring lodged in its belly?

This morning I was awoken by twenty-one cannon shots. The citadel was saluting the docking of a Navy training ship that I had spotted arriving yesterday from Dutch Guiana. Young Nordic men fill the streets, their faces crimsoned by the Tropics, their uniforms bristling with insignia. The bars are playing 'Valencia' for these (drunken) sailors. I've been trying in vain to find Negro bands but the only instruments played here are wind-up keyboards. All the women are outdoors, the coloured women I mean, of course. Indeed, I've only come across two white women in Curaçao. In the evenings, looking through the open windows and doors one can see indolent individuals of mixed race seated in rocking chairs on their verandas. Behind them, drawing-rooms painted in blue and green are lit up by chandeliers of Venetian crystal and decorated with imported kakemonos.[84]

Travelling around Curaçao is extremely expensive because of the bridges and the tolls that have to be paid in florins. Also, if the bridges have opened to let boats through, one must then resort to the ferries, which are even more costly. I shall leave Curaçao beggared by the bridges.

At four o'clock I board the boat that will take three days to bring me to Port-au-Prince.

---

83 Janissaries were fourteenth to sixteenth-century Turkish infantry soldiers of the Sultan's personal guard. Their uniform included tall helmets or hats.

84 These are unframed Japanese wall-hangings or scrolls.

What I like about ports is the fact that they have no nationality. They always take on the nationality of the last ship to dock there. Yesterday Curaçao was Dutch; the previous day, American; and the day before that, it was French.

NOVEMBER 29TH AND 30TH

We've been hit by an east wind blowing diagonally across the Caribbean Sea and so here I am – once again – with my head stuck in a basin. Having unloaded all the merchandise from its hold in Curaçao our cargo ship had become too light for the heavy seas and was lurching about in the swell. Since my cabin was at the back of the ship beside the propeller, every wave bashed us like a baseball bat, making me hop about like one of the villagers made a fool of by the old crones depicted in Goya's tapestries. It was dreadful! The stars in the porthole were falling like shooting stars one minute, only to rise up like rockets the next and the entire sky was wheeling round the earth and diving under the boat. We clambered up on deck using our hands more than our feet, while the wind that cut through us burned our skin and slapped us about, tearing off our clothes.

DECEMBER 1ST

The resilience of the human body is extraordinary. That's why there is a world of difference between being seasick and being shipwrecked. This morning here I am, freshly showered, tucking into a delicious Dutch breakfast. We spend the entire morning sailing around inside the Bay of Haiti. Haiti is an enormous island, the largest of the West Indies with the exception of Cuba. As everyone knows, the Indies get smaller and smaller from the north-west to the south-east, eventually dwindling into invisibility.

CARIBBEAN WINTER

DECEMBER 2ND

We arrived in Haiti towards 5 p.m.. The Chancellor of our embassy was waiting for me and he had been joined on the spur of the moment by M. L., a Haitian poet and author of a book on the personal life of Maurice Rostand.[85] Avant-garde Haitian literature, from the blackest to the palest, has come on board to greet me in person and to hand me the morning newspaper, in which I'm dubbed a 'young Giant of the Literary World'.

I'm brought to the home of the French ambassador. He's a pleasant man who shares his life with some eighty travel trunks. Though he has been here for a few months already, he hasn't been able even to start unpacking. He finds the climate unbearable and is tearing his hair out because there's no sign of a posting to somewhere else. He gives me a warm welcome tinged with a certain apprehension: 'Within a couple of days you'll have seen everything that there is to see here. Though actually there's nothing to see.' He appeals for confirmation of this to the author[86] of the book on Maurice Rostand, who is breathing down our necks.

The Haitians are all wondering what I'm going to write about them. Paul Reboux[87] made an enduring impression here. Indeed, the islanders have never forgiven him for having caricatured them. 'So Mr Paul Morand is to pay us a visit?' the president apparently said to our ambassador. 'How unfortunate that his name is Paul, *just like that other fellow.*' Ah yes, Reboux, Haiti remembers you very well.

---

85 Maurice Rostand (1891-1968 and son of Edmond Rostand, author of *Cyrano de Bergerac*) was a writer of poems, novels and plays.

86 This reference concerns Léon Laleau (1892-1979), the Haitian novelist, poet, journalist and diplomat who authored *Maurice Rostand, intime* (Paris: Éditions du monde moderne, 1926).

87 André Amillet, who used the pseudonym Paul Reboux (1877-1963) was the author of *Le Paradis des Antilles françaises*, Paris: Librairie de la Revue française (Toutes nos colonies), 1931. He was a prolific novelist who excelled in pastiche.

I'm now in the South of the island. On arriving in a place populated by Negroes, one gets the same impression as when one has just left an English country for a Latin land. The porters are busy insulting one another and begging for money; the man in the street has nothing better to do than to scrutinize you, while the customs officers – drunk with self-importance – routinely push you around. Meanwhile, verbose journalists, scarcely more dark-skinned than the Southerners of Europe, play billiards with their rivals, turning a blind eye to the daily insults involved. Given that the editorial of today's newspaper (*Le Nouvelliste*) is attacking the president about a fire hydrant, it's clear that the press here is no less devoid of world news, no less parochial than the *Tarascon Beacon* or the *Little Narbonnais*. Haitians love the French nineteenth century because it holds up a mirror to their own history: caciquism[88], romantic riots, military coups, etc.

- So what do you think of Haiti?, I'm asked.

- Well, nothing as of yet. But it seems to me that a compressed time-span, no more than one hundred years, will separate the beautiful French eighteenth-century colony from the powerful twentieth-century American empire that will prevail here in the future. After all, throughout the entire nineteenth century the Blacks have, unfortunately, shown no aptitude for founding a stable political regime.

'All I can say, Sir,' a Haitian lawyer tells me, 'is that I invited Reboux to dinner along with one of my friends who is a general. And afterwards Reboux wrote: "After dinner the general began to sing, tapping the beat with his bare toes." Well, Sir, that was not so at all, for the general did, of course, have his boots on. What's more, the Haitians, who like their boots to be well polished, are deeply offended, not just by the sight of people going about barefoot on their streets, but also when this practice is pointed out.'

---

88 The word *cacique* is derived from a Taino word used in the pre-Columbian world of the Caribbean for example, to mean indigenous chief. *Caciquismo* or caciquism can be translated as 'warlordism' or 'boss rule'.

Many writers who travel to other places are thus criticized for repaying with odious observations the warm welcome that they receive abroad. But the fact is that the said welcome is often imposed on the writers in question. In reality, the latter are approached and put upon by their hosts, who impose on them a programme that's nothing short of propaganda. Then, when they're sceptical, they are accused of betrayal. I myself was at pains not to seek any letter of introduction to Haiti. Rather than going along in person to the Haitian embassy in Paris, I had my passport brought there for me. I was thus careful to travel on my own steam, accepting no favours that might subsequently be used as ammunition. And I did so quite deliberately, in order to be free to say whatever I pleased. Indeed, when the president let me know that he intended to receive me (though he withdrew the invitation almost immediately), I had no option but to accept an audience that I had never sought.

Beneath the straight grey pillars of the palm-trees, whole families confuse outdoor lamplight with sunshine, taking to the shade at night. American gramophones are playing for them fake Negro tunes that nobody recognizes, but that nonetheless find favour here because they are mistakenly regarded as music for Whites. 'Marines' and 'Sammies'[89] drink in a polychrome bar called 'Mo'martre'. Small carriages drawn by scrawny ponies alert us to their presence with a clamorous ringing of bells.

I now learn that the reason why the president, Mr Borno, cancelled our meeting was because some friendly spy had shown him a sentence from *Rien que la terre*[90] in which I make reference to 'dirty half-castes'. Mr Borno, who is particularly prickly, at once declared himself a half-caste and mortally offended as such by my words.

---

89 From 'Uncle Sam', the nickname given to the US in the war of independence, around 1812. The term was used in recruitment posters and applied by extension as 'Sammie' to depictions of American soldiers in the British or French media.

90 *Rien que la terre* (Naught Save the Earth) was published in 1926 and recounts Morand's 1925 journey to the Far East. See above, p. 2.

It so happens, however, that I had not written 'the age of the dirty half-caste', but rather the 'dirty age of the half-caste'. Black and white are both beautiful; what's ugly is grey.

It was in 1915 that a president of Haiti was assassinated at the French embassy despite the tradition of diplomatic asylum. Since France could not intervene, the Americans jumped on this opportunity to occupy the Western part of the island, that is, the Haitian Republic[91]. They then tried to establish their dominion in the East as well but the Spanish Mulattoes of Santo Domingo, who are less passive than the Negroes of Haiti, protested in Europe and even threatened to revolt, whereupon the American Navy withdrew back to the West.

The present government is opportunistic and has resigned itself for the moment to the American occupation. This suits the president well enough because it means that he can stay in power indefinitely. It's six years since he last called a sitting of parliament. The Haitian constitution is an imitation of ours, with the slight difference that the State Council replaces both the upper and the lower houses of parliament since, just like our Popular Assembly or lower house, it votes in legislation, but it also ratifies it, just like our Senate. The Haitian State Council also acts as a Constitutional Assembly by appointing the president, for example. The president returns the favour by nominating the twelve members of the State Council. As for the opposition, it

---

91 Vibrun Guillaume Sam (1859-1915) was the fifth Haitian President to hold power in a single five-year period (he presided over Haiti for just five months, from February 25 to July 28, 1915). He succeeded Joseph Davilrar Théodore who had been unable to pay the militia (the *Cacos*), who had helped him to overthrow the previous regime (of President Zamor). Sam struggled, however, to control opposition from within his own regime, which was unhappy with the strategy of rapprochement to the USA. Eventually, he had about 150 of his opponents executed, including his precursor's precursor, Zamor. In the ensuing chaos, he was lynched, whereupon President Woodrow Wilson, fearing a replacement regime hostile to US interests, ordered American troops into Haiti. The American occupation continued for nineteen years, until August 1934.

has to make do with looking after fines and imprisonment. The journalist with whom we are dining this evening was imprisoned a short while ago and was released only because the wife of the president of the neighbouring state – the Dominican Republic – allegedly asked for him to be pardoned on the basis of his famous good looks.

Upon my return from the embassy, I received a visit from the two directors of the *Revue indigène*, Haiti's avant-garde literary journal. Valéry Larbaud[92] had spoken to me about one of them. Together they have dreamed up an admirable project: self-emancipation from that blind imitation of French literature that has been such a soporific and debilitating brake on the development of Haitian poetry. Instead, they want to bring an original Haitian perspective to bear on the world. Already they are writing things like: 'Fingers entwined for a dance around the whole world'. They themselves should beware, however, of falling into the trap of copying Apollinaire, Max Jacob or Cendrars, in the same way that their ancestors used to parrot Béranger or Casimir Delavigne[93].

The Haitian newspaper *L'Information* features a review of the speech made yesterday by an Italian journalist at a press conference in Port-au-Prince. This peddler of fascist propaganda expressed his contempt for French civilization in Indochina, calling it a 'stage set made of cardboard and silk that will collapse at the first storm'.

---

92 Valéry Larbaud (1881–1957) was a much-travelled, cosmopolitan French writer whose family owned the spa-water source of Vichy St Yorre. Larbaud is mainly known as a novelist and for having supervised the French translation of Joyce's *Ulysses*.

93 Guillaume Apollinaire, Max Jacob and Blaise Cendrars were Modernist, Cubist and urban poets whose writing was influential in the first decades of the twentieth century and far beyond them. Casimir Delavigne (1793-1843) was a best-selling and influential French poet and dramatist whose fame did not travel into the twentieth century; similarly, Pierre-Jean de Béranger (1780-1857) was a prolific poet and *chansonnier*, but his great success and popularity in his own time did not long survive him either.

Some charming Blacks, very light-skinned, have invited me to dine with them on the waterfront at the Franco-Haitian tennis club. They are naturally bald and have big cheeks, along with beards, opinions, gold watches, snobbery, indignation and solid digestion systems. There was no need to travel so far to find this. For there's nothing exotic about this company, at least not on the surface. My companions are most urbane. They read *Le Canard enchaîné* and *Le Merle blanc*[94] and inquire of me what was really behind a duel that I never even heard of, between one Pierre Brisson and a son of Richepin.[95] They make me listen to a *méringue*[96], a Haitian dance tune rather half-heartedly composed by a student of our own Conservatoire and all dressed up in a sauce of virtuosity and skill. For his part, the journalist regales us with tales of his time as a political prisoner. All of Port-au Prince had brought him cigars in his prison cell; ladies too had called upon him and his jailor had come by each morning to collect his copy for the evening newspaper.

In the outdoor markets, hundreds of women crouched on their hunkers are selling little piles of charcoal, fistfuls of corn, black seaweed, empty gourds. From these enormous Negresses emanate ridiculously tiny voices. Other women pass by with an air of great self-assurance, bearing piles of minute green chili peppers on their heads.

A housewife stands in pink stockings; she has one shoe on her foot and is holding the other in her hand.

94　These are the titles of two satirical French (weekly) newspapers, the former of which is still in existence. *Le Merle blanc* was founded in 1919 by Eugène Merle and was selling 800,000 copies per week by the time that its founder launched the daily newspaper, *France-Soir*, in 1923.

95　Pierre Brisson was a journalist and director of *Le Figaro* newspaper; Jean Richepin, who died in 1926, was a French poet born in Algeria.

96　The *méringue* is a Haitian dance originating in the nineteenth century. Unlike the Dominican *merengue*, with which it is often confused, its music is string- rather than accordion-based.

CARIBBEAN WINTER

On the shopfronts, the terms 'Wholesale' and 'Retail' are rendered as 'Grossness' and 'Finesse'.

I pay an afternoon visit to the parish priest of Port-au-Prince, a Frenchman. He shows me a Christ's head washed up by the sea. According to the rules of voodoo ritual, the sorcerer or *papaloi*[97] must throw an object of Catholic devotion into the sea. No Whites are allowed to be present at the magic ceremonies and, after they have dispersed, the celebrants never speak of what they have seen or done. When an evil fetish is found on the threshold of a house, the inhabitants stay inside and don't dare emerge for days. Sometimes they go so far as to demolish the whole house.

The Archbishop, Monsignor C., has been officiating in Port-au-Prince for forty years. He has a fine hairy face and compassionate eyes. The priests and religious who work abroad remain frozen in the past, as though they've been put on ice. They seem to carry the seventeenth century around with them. Not only do they share the language, culture and features of the people of that era, but they show great spontaneity of feeling, an absence of modern febrility and a total ignorance of our current epoch, both of its beauties and of its blemishes. The French priests and nuns of the foreign missions and especially those of the Far-East and African missions, are the loveliest specimens of old-style human morality that I've ever had the privilege of encountering.

Soldiers conquer the colonies for us; priests educate them; administrators organize them; tourists disfigure them; businessmen ruin them and politicians surrender them.

Mr. L. L. comes to collect me after dinner. We go for a walk in the hills, above Peu-de-Chose, in the American quarter. The lawns there look like padded upholstery, the zinc roofs shine in the moonlight and the sky has been rubbed with graphite dust. The tall pillars of the palm trees are grooved and the verandas are as spacious as the decks of ships. The sound of gramophones rings out. Then silence. Stars twinkle and crickets call. In the

---

97 *Papaloi* is the name given to a male voodoo priest, especially in Haiti.

distance the sea is devoid of masts. We enter an elegant dancehall where people are dancing the *méringue*. The ladies are almost all dressed in pink. Their skin is the colour of gold, honey, mahogany, cocoa or cinchona bark.[98] They don't wear their hair straightened as they do in America, nor with large partings like Josephine Baker's.[99] The Negro fashions of Haiti don't come from Harlem, but rather take a detour through Paris: straight lines don't come naturally to Haitians.

The Spaniards were met by two different indigenous races. In the North, and especially in Haiti, they encountered the Arawaks. In the South, in the Lesser Antilles, they came upon the Caribs, or Cannibals.

'It is in the nature of Blacks to be drawn to absolutes, to be easy to enslave and happy to follow, herd-like, abstract ideas. They do not require the latter to be comprehensible, for they prefer to fear and obey rather than to understand.' This is the definition of black nature offered by Gobineau's *The Inequality of Human Races*. And this is why all civilizations tinged with melanin must be governed by despotism.

DECEMBER 4TH

Mr C. tells me that the most felicitous interbreeding in Haiti was that of the French with the so-called *poulards*, a group of

---

98 The dried bark of the Chincona tree contains quinine and is the colour of cinnamon.

99 Josephine Baker was a very famous African American born into poverty and deprivation in Saint-Louis, Missouri. She was married twice before she was 17 and it was her second husband's name that she retained all her life. Her talent as an entertainer was spotted in the USA and when she moved to France she had a glittering career as a dancer and singer in Paris. She married two different French men, associated herself with the Résistance in the war years in France and with the Civil Rights movement in the US in the early sixties. She adopted a dozen children from all over the world as a 'rainbow family' gesture of resistance towards racism and discrimination. The French people took her to their heart.

Negroes from the province of Jérémie[100]. The Dumas[101] family came from Jérémie.

The harbour of Port-au-Prince is home to one solitary shark, a cunning old fellow who lost an eye in the war against mankind and who cannot be captured. He's called after a former Haitian president.

Before lunch, C. and one of his friends take me into the countryside to a cockfight. I enter a circular pit four or five metres in diameter with an earthen floor. In the centre a large stake, resembling the central spoke of an umbrella, holds up a

100 See Rebecca J. Scott, 'Rosalie of the Poulard Nation: Freedom, Law, and Dignity in the Era of the Haitian Revolution', in *Assumed Identities: The Meanings of Race in the Atlantic World*, ed. J. D. Garrigus and C. Morris, 116-43. Walter Prescott Webb Memorial Lectures, 41. College Station, Texas: Texas A&M Univ. Press, 2010. According to Scott, the 'term "Poulard" [...] referred to speakers of Pulaar, and by extension to the group generally called Peul in French and Fulbe in English. [Rosalie] had evidently been made a captive years before, somewhere in the broad area across which the Peul had migrated, extending from the Senegal River valley to the upper Guinea coast and inland to Mali and beyond.' The Haitian 'Rosalie' of whom Scott writes 'may have been purchased in the Galam trade, the annual convoy of boats that travelled upriver from the West African island port of Saint-Louis du Sénégal to exchange textiles, paper, and other merchandise for gum Arabic (used in textile processing) and captives'. p. 118. The classic description of the individual parishes of the colony is that of Médéric Moreau de Saint-Méry, *Description topographique, physique, civil, politique et historique de la partie française de l'isle de Saint-Domingue*, reprint ed. ([1797] Paris: Société Française d'Histoire d'Outre-Mer, 2004.

101 The grandmother of the novelist Alexandre Dumas Sr was a slave on the de Pailletterie plantation La Guinaudée near Jérémie in Haiti. Her name was Marie-Cessette Dumas and she bore the plantation-owner four children, the youngest of whom and his father's favourite, Thomas-Alexandre, was brought to France in 1775, where he eventually took his mother's name. Thomas-Alexandre Dumas was the father of Alexandre Dumas, *père* (1802-1870), the famous novelist and author of *The Three Musketeers* (1844) and *The Count of Monte Cristo* (1845). He was the grandfather of Alexandre Dumas, *fils* (1824-1895), the dramatist (and author of *La Dame aux camélias*, which was published in 1848).

roof of poorly-spaced dried palms through which the sunlight penetrates in spots. The sky is blue and the landscape outside is green, with skinny cows grazing like a frieze of horses. Behind a circular rail are four tiered rows of black faces, all belonging to humble folk. A 'high society' Black would lose status if he attended a cockfight, called a *gagaire* (from the Latin word *gallus*, meaning cockerel). The Negroes wear white, khaki or American denim overalls, with wide braces in cotton twill and big straw hats called 'plantation hats'. In the top row some little boys are standing between the men's spread legs, while others are hanging from the roof by bare, black arms that are knotted like gnarled roots. The owners take bets while the 'healers' wait in the neighbouring café holding their cock under their arm. Inside the circle that forms the ring are a couple of chairs reserved for the VIPs, who are like the great noblemen at Molière's plays. The cocks are skinny, still and red-eyed. The cockadoodledoos of other cocks awaiting their turn nearby seem to rouse them like a challenge; no fighting cock will allow another cock to crow anywhere close to him.

An English Jew from Jamaica is pointed out to me as having managed to lay his hands on the best fighters in all of the Caribbean. He owns cocks worth three or even four hundred dollars. Sometimes the country folk arrive with a champion in which they've bought shares and invested all their hopes. But the Jamaican's cocks always win because they are trained more scientifically. They are made to cycle with their feet for an hour every day to make them more supple and their skin and feathers are hardened with ginger so that the blows just glance off their wings. Nobody dares stand against them. Today, the chief challenger belongs to a Chinese launderer.

The show is about to begin. Already the owners are sharpening the birds' spurs with a penknife. They lick the spurs, pointed like steel, to show the spectators that they haven't been poisoned. Then, from cheeks swollen with water they spray the cock's head, inducing the bird to emerge from its lethargy like a boxer. A space is immediately cleared and the contestants face each other. From that moment onwards it's a fight to the death, unless the wounded fighter is 'lifted' (i.e. withdrawn). The fight can last an hour or a minute, but for the entire duration the cocks won't leave one another alone. They follow each other so closely with their beaks that one could well imagine that there is only one of them moving in front of a mirror. They peck each other in the eyes and in the crest and between the wings; they sink their spurs into each other's flesh. Some of them have secret boots like fencers. The cock belonging to the Jew is a seasoned old pugilist. He starts running around in circles to tire out his adversary. The latter, who doesn't understand this ploy, exhausts himself keeping up. All of a sudden, secure in his own strength, the strategist turns and pounces on the amateur bumpkin who is by now out of breath. The punters roar and stand up on their chairs as soon as the fighters approach them, for the rules of the game dictate that the birds cannot be touched during the duel. When one of the contestants gains an advantage the odds rise immediately. The punters taunt and threaten each other, brandishing fistfuls of dollars or dirty gourds. 'Ten dollars.' 'Fifteen dollars.' 'You're on.' The punter crosses the arena. But in the meantime his bird has just been wounded. That makes him cautious: the bet is off and the stakes are returned to his pocket.

Meanwhile, as the Chinaman eggs on the challenger, the Jamaican encourages his champion with words and gestures. The two cocks, cut to ribbons, have turned into bleeding balls: their beaks hang open, they are panting and their hearts are beating as though they would burst. Yet they are both hanging on like two exhausted boxers, each one leaning on the adversary's shoulder, their crests swollen and their heads blackened... Finally one of them weakens. He lies down and only gets up when attacked. He's going to die. To save his life, his owner picks him up from behind (with some treatment, in a week he'll look fine and will be able to fight again). He's been withdrawn.

We travel up to Pétionville[102] to have lunch high in the *mornes* or mountains at six hundred metres. The air here is delicious, like spring water. The houses are cool and look out on the bay and on the mountains. Here, the natural world is nothing like that depicted by the miser Veronese[103], a man too mean to pay the price of going overseas to find inspiration. Having been uprooted from African soil, the Negroes have taken root again and seem happy here. These Caribbean dungeons have been transformed from open-air prisons for slaves into places of luxury and entertainment. There's even an ice-cold swimming pool.

As luck would have it we're not far away from the president's villa where I've been invited for four o'clock. Some of the guests are related to the president but these are actually his worst enemies. 'It's precisely because I'm his cousin that he's so quick to have me put in prison', C. – the journalist – tells me.

We enjoy a lovely Creole meal, *ti-malice* sauce[104], guava chutney, avocados with smoked herring, white rice, sweet potato… The entire repast is misted in the deafening spray of the sparkling wines. There's a whole host of bubblies: a sparkling Burgundy, a fizzy Saumur and an effervescent Asti! All the finest wines of the world have been mixed with sugar, spirits and carbonic acid. As for the cocktails, they are made with Haitian rum, said to be the best in the Caribbean and priced at up to three hundred francs a bottle. To finish off the occasion we are served the locally famous coffee. It's very sweet, very black and packs an extraordinary punch despite its velvety smoothness. It's

---

102 Pétionville is a largely affluent highland suburb of Port-au-Prince, named after one of the four founding fathers of Haiti: the general and president, Alexandre Sabès Pétion (1770-1818). The other three historical figures were Jean-Jacques Dessalines, Henry Christophe and Toussaint Louverture.

103 Veronese, born Bonifacio de Pitati in Verona, was an Italian Renaissance painter, 1487-1553.

104 *Sauce à la petite malice*, called sauce ti-malice in Creole (literally 'little mischief sauce'), is a typically Haitian, tomato-based accompaniment to fish and meat dishes.

used to sweeten Brazilian coffee, which is overly bitter. This is the plant, growing right here. I've only just now discovered that this small red berry, this tiny kernel, is in fact the coffee grain.

Our provincial luncheon, relished as Parisians were falling asleep in the snow, was a simple but delightful illustration of the joy of being alive. The good spirits of these middle-class Haitians make of them the spitting image of our own French bourgeoisie. Their sense of humour, their stories – so pungent and droll – the epicureanism of their lifestyle, their worship of good food and drink, all of this comes straight from France.

'Do you remember when we were at the *lycée* Stanislas[105], in Composition Class…?'

We finally leave the table at half-past four. I've let myself be stuffed like a bird and in just a few moments I'll be having an audience with the president.

'There will be no more fun and games once we're in my cousin's company,' the journalist tells me. And when I start worrying about how I'm going to get to the presidential residence, my host replies: 'I'll bring you there in my car. But I'll wait for you at the gate as I'm no longer on speaking terms with that fellow.'

True enough, it's all pomp and ceremony. At the gate of the presidential palace an official is dressed in a khaki uniform, which includes a large Turkish-style cape.[106] On the veranda stands the president himself, a tall Mulatto of Guadeloupean origin, a fine figure of a man, his posture maintained erect by the sharp cut of his American jacket. He's wearing gold-rimmed glasses and his hair is white. With measured, automatic gestures he hands me some Havana cigars, the best I've ever smoked. As he begins to speak with practised ease, telling me that he has just cancelled a planned trip to the Dominican Republic because of the hostility of the local press, I can see that he likes the sound of his own voice.

---

105 This private and prestigious Catholic *lycée* is located in the Montparnasse district of Paris and was founded in 1804.
106 A Turkish-style robe with cape-like sleeves.

'Believe me, dear Sir, to be entirely well-disposed towards the freedom of the press. You can take it that I'm all in favour of it. But within limits, of course, and these limits are dictated by the interests of public opinion. I cannot allow a few fractious elements (etc…).'

President Borno[107] sings the praises of peace and tranquillity, but also of prosperity – that reliable guarantee of national happiness. Intoning a (slightly disguised) hymn in praise of strong-arm tactics, he makes no effort to hide his view that the foreign occupation, although ever so painful to patriots, is a political necessity. He is haughty, warm and every bit the 'sovereign'.

'I'm all for the iron glove in the velvet hand. I'm opposed to harshness, in favour of firmness whenever possible, but draconian when required. Fair and lawful punishment should not be confused with torture. Nobody is tortured in Haiti, at least not since French colonial times. Did you ever hear of Colonel Rochambeau? This was the man who invited Haitian women to a funeral dance. Rows of corpses were hidden behind black drapes and these included the ladies' own husbands who had been shot while their wives were dancing. And then think, Sir, of the terrible crimes, including cannibalism, that are committed in Europe and in the United States. Remember the Hanover Butcher! You must have heard of him … or the Italian who ate the hearts of his victims? It's not so long ago since a club for cannibals was discovered in New York, counting

---

107 Eustache Antoine François Joseph Louis Borno (1865-1942) was president of Haiti between 1922 and 1930, coming to power seven seven years after the American Occupation began. The end of his term coincided with the end of the Occupation. A Paris-educated lawyer, he was the son of a white French father and black Haitian mother. His impressive record of successful reforms and improvements (especially in infrastructure and education, but also in national debt management) was enabled by strategic collaboration with the Americans, though it was marked by a democratic deficit (Borno refused to hold free elections).

among its members a girl who had drunk human blood. Ah, here is the American High Commissioner and his wife, Mrs Russel[108], who have come to tea. Oh no, don't leave us, do please stay on!'

The general's wife was extremely agreeable and we found that we have some friends in common. However, no amount of formal politeness could hide the deep, implacable and absolute contempt for coloured people shown by the American dignitary himself. Champagne!

The general owns a villa in Deauville where he spends six months each year. He has just come back from a visit there and is impatient to return. More champagne!

Evening falls on the mountains as the moon rises. It's no longer possible to see people's faces. In fact, nothing is visible now except the white linen jackets. Since the High Commissioner made his entrance, the president has uttered not a single word. An icy protocol prevails. The cockfight and the lunch beneath the marquee seem very far away from us now.

This morning, the editors of the *Revue indigène*[109] collected me and drove me thirty kilometres away from Port-au-Prince, to a plantation belonging to one of their fathers, but formerly owned by an aristocrat of the *ancien régime*. In Haiti, there are still farms bearing names like Rohan-Montbazon, Noailles,

---

108 Major General John Henry Russell Jr (1872-1947) was a much-decorated American Navy officer. Having served in the Dominican Republic, then Haiti, between 1917 and 1918, he requested a transfer from the Caribbean just as the war was ending. Given his eminence, his subsequent appointment by the president in 1922 as American High Commissioner in Haiti (ranked as Ambassador Extraordinary) is held by historians to prove the perceived strategic importance of Haiti for the US administration. He was to serve in this capacity during the entire term of President Borno (until November 1930).

109 The *Revue indigène* was a Haitian literary journal founded in 1927. Its ethos was based on the anti-colonial ideas of local cultural authenticity developed by the Haitian ethnologist Jean Price-Mars. There were six monthly issues in all, between 1927 and 1928.

Montmorency[110]. In fact, the Haitian plantations were very lucrative for the big French families of the *ancien régime*. After the Revolution, their estates were distributed among the black soldiers of the Haitian Republic.

The young men accompanying me are all aged between nineteen and twenty-three and belong to the Haitian bourgeoisie. They come from many different backgrounds and boast varying degrees of intelligence. They include lawyers, students and future politicians, but are all unpretentious, charming and very mannerly.

The plantation that we're to visit lies at the foot of the mountains. After a very fast drive, we find ourselves in an irrigated plain, planted with wonderful sugar cane three metres tall. High above it passes an old French aqueduct, surrounded by laurel trees in flower. Two small grey donkeys are grazing on the void in the shade of a plastered pavilion, itself opening onto a terrace that is propped up by stakes. We sit down to drink some iced rum on the only patch of ground for miles that is sheltered from the sun. The landscape is peaceful and noble and recalls the Euganean Hills.[111] The time whiled away among these young men dressed in white is a languid, lazy spell spent pondering in the limpid light questions and answers reminiscent of the Socratic dialogues. One of the young men is very handsome and resembles a Cuban gentleman. Another is more rustic in appearance. Still another, who is both very black and very pleasant, has big bloodshot eyes and two small front teeth sticking out of his mouth; his gums, like those of the bear in Rimbaud's *Illuminations*, are purple, and his tongue is as pink as a fruit pastille. These young Haitian intellectuals are interested in everything and they are proud and intense. They particularly

---

110 These are all French toponyms associated with particular aristocratic families.

111 The Euganean Hills are of volcanic origin and are located near Padua in Italy.

admire Montherlant and also Delteil.[112] They are astounded by Max Jacob[113] but are quite divided on the subject of surrealism, though they don't completely understand what it's about. Passionately patriotic to a man, they all detest the Americans and enjoy working each other up on the matter: Ah, if only we had arms! They are strikingly different from their forebears in all things with the single exception of their predilection for France. Like all post-war nationalisms, Chinese, Mexican, Turkish, etc., theirs is extreme. They adore their country, its history and its customs, and they respond with good grace to my questions on voodoo. Yes, they themselves have been present at ceremonies where Negresses dressed in white were positioned around fires. One of these had once woken up another woman who had been hypnotized and who seemed to my interlocutor to be coming back from somewhere else. As she returned to her senses, she cried out 'I'm leaving, I'm on my way', before opening her eyes and announcing 'I'm here.'

DECEMBER 6TH

I've been here in Haiti for a fortnight already. I'm afraid that I missed two good opportunities to get away and there is no sign of another boat. Am I going to turn Haitian? It's impossible to get to Kingston, Jamaica, to Santiago de Cuba or to Havana. This is why we need to beware of islands: the newspapers here in Port-au-Prince announce the arrival of steamers three days after they've already been and gone. I've had my fill by now of the palm trees, the sunsets, the Negroes and the blue sky. All the poets of Port-au-Prince are kindly sending me their work and a magistrate has written to ask me to intercede with the Haitian courts.

---

112 Montherlant, see note 32. Joseph Delteil (1894-1978) was a French writer and poet, who did not belong to any particular school or tradition and authored about forty books.

113 Max Jacob, see note 93.

I pay a visit to Brother S., who is a teacher in a large French secondary school in Port-au-Prince. He's the very picture of 'primitive man': all simplicity and goodness. This man of God travels the island on horseback, supporting the priests marooned high up in the mountains and visiting the eighteen schools within his remit. Everyone who knows how to read and write has passed through the hands of our religious, who are cherished and respected by the Haitians. These Christian brothers are saints. As they've been here on their own up to now, they've been able to get close to the natives and the primitive races. Their secret is simple: they love the people and they themselves lead exemplary lives. 'Nobody can have the slightest influence on the Negroes,' writes Livingstone[114], 'unless his own morals are beyond reproach and unless he is of loyal character. All of a foreigner's actions are minutely scrutinized and each native brings to this scrutiny a depth of insight that is rarely found wanting.'

This evening, I'm invited, along with the brigadier general of the police force and the chief medical officer and his wife, to a private dinner at the residence of the American High Commissioner in Haiti. It's a fine colonial-style house with red-brick verandas overlooking both the bay and the city. The latter is lit up by the red beam from the cathedral, while the full moon is shining down on the even more phosphorescent Caribbean Sea. In the garden, the white uniforms and bluish-white dinner jackets gleam through the dark shapes of the black mango trees. The scene is reminiscent of the spectacle provided by the British Army in India. American soldiers in khaki stand to attention behind the table. However, the American colonial brigade lacks the elegance of the professional German or English officers. Even though they have excellent deportment, they look like civilians dressed up as military men. We drink nothing but water.

114 Dr David Livingstone (1813-1873) was a medical missionary and explorer of Scottish origin. His aim of discovering the sources of the Nile was subordinated to the greater objective of wiping out slavery in Africa through the development of 'enlightened' colonial commerce.

Although it's the middle of December, the fans are whirring out on the verandas beneath the open galleries of the upper floors. In their white timber houses, which are all clustered together in a quarter called 'Peu-de-Chose' (Nothing Much), the American officers are listening to Roxy Radio broadcasting from New York. The rooms are bare, quite devoid of solid furnishings. There is much here, however, to remind me of Shanghai: along with the darkness outside on the verandas, there are the cocktail-shakers, the Chinese rugs, the pianos, the cane tables and chairs and the saddles in the ante-chamber.

In Haiti, nobody would dream of charging for favours; everywhere, people help each other out.

Many American agricultural companies have gone bankrupt in Haiti because they wanted to do things the Californian or Hawaiian or Filipino way. But when it came to ploughing, digging canals and harvesting, they were obliged to revert to age-old French ways. The Blacks have kept alive all the traditional know-how for growing pineapples and have been able to develop and apply it most impressively right across the island.

In the afternoon, I take a delightful trip out to Mirebalais[115] with Monsieur Chevalier, the Director of Posts and Telegraphs. Monsieur Chevalier shakes everybody's hand; he's the unofficial go-between linking government and opposition. In other words, he's the director of propaganda, the most amiable of intermediaries and the most precious of guides.

We travel through the mountains along a rocky road pierced by the occasional aloe plant. This route runs high above the great plain of Port-au-Prince, officially known as the plain of Cul-de-Sac, which extends as far the lake of saltpetre separating Haiti from the Dominican Republic.

Six hundred metres below us the countryside stretches out in the great green squares formed by the plantations of sugar

---

115 Mirebalais is a city in the centre of Haiti, about sixty kilometres from the capital. It was founded in 1702.

cane. There is blue smoke in the air as the sun sets behind Petit-Goâve (Lesser Guava), one of those quaint Haitian place names like Adieu-au-Monde (Farewell, World), Grand-Gosier (Great Gizzard), Marché-Canard (Walking Duck)[116], Moka-Neuf (New Mokka), Jamais-Vu (Unheard Of), Dondon (Big Fat Momma), Sale-Trou (Dirty Hole) and most especially, Lemonade or Marmelade, derisory toponyms given by the first French settlers to the marshy territories around Cap-Haïtien, territories that Emperor Soulouque[117] would later turn into dukedoms. At the gap of Terre-Rouge, we take tea in a police station where the territorial army offers us hospitality. American officers have left their mark: none of your flea-infested straw mattresses here. Instead, there are folding metal bedframes hanging two-by-two in v-formation, with the mattresses laid outdoors in the sun for disinfection. We come across prisoners moving from one village to another in their striped convict uniforms. Having volunteered for day missions, they travel without an escort and, the following day, they will return to their prison cells of their own free will.

Just like in Africa, we see a lot of donkeys. All the Negroes are clad in blue cotton, the women adding a yellow cotton kerchief knotted around their heads, the men sporting wide plantation hats, pulled down as far as the gold rings in their ears. On their heads they carry gourds as smooth and as black as the heads that bear them.

We return home late; the open-air markets are still trading and remain open far into the night. Each vendor is crouching, immobile, on the ground and they are all lit up by a small lamp

---

116 The derivation of this toponym is anybody's guess: *marché* could mean 'market' and history records that a landowner named Canard held a plantation in Haiti (his ownership is attested both in the 1742 Lebrun map and also in the 1786 Phelipeau survey).

117 Faustin-Elie Soulouque (1782-1867), an army general, was elected president in 1847, He became Emperor Faustin I two years later, establishing a black nobility and a personal militia. His failed attempts to extend his power to the Dominican Republic undermined his authority and he had to abdicate in 1859.

whose flame is bending in the wind. Behind these lamps, their faces recede into the shade; the only bright feature are the big staring eyes inlaid with white above flattened noses: cat faces.

If there is still so much magic in the Caribbean islands, a priest tells me, it's because the Negroes have been taught that the 'Christian God is good' and so there is no need to pray to Him; as a result they prefer to adore the devil.

Sweat in hot countries is not disgusting. It doesn't have the acrid, sour, unwashed smell of sweat in cold countries. Instead it's a natural function, like the liquid breath of the skin.

The Americans, I'm told, showed extreme brutality in putting down the 1920 rising in Haiti, using toxic gases and air-bombing against the civil population. It certainly seems clear that the mode of repression was disproportionate to the strength of the revolt. Of course, the same practice is observed in the United States, where it can happen that officers on motorcycles, protected by a line of shields, will use tanks, canons, revolvers or machine guns to arrest one single miscreant.

I'm struck by the indifference of the Negroes towards white women. Yet for me, they never were those satyrs or gorillas that the American newspapers made them out to be.

I spend the day in the Seaside Inn, by the sea. It's a large detached building, standing all alone on a white coral strand fringed with drooping coconut trees and coral branches as tall as the antlers of a mature deer. After lunch, there's a siesta in one of those wonderful, ever so flexible, unknotted Venezuelan hammocks, which fold up into the size of a handkerchief.

Towards evening my young friends come to the Inn for a cocktail. I've adopted this place as my daytime base, returning every night to sleep in the city. One of my young companions has the flat hair and beautiful liquid eyes of a Ceylonese face and they are all, to a man, full of passion and enthusiasm. They cannot stop telling heroic tales of Haiti's civil wars and its struggle for independence. Without an instant's hesitation, they place Toussaint Louverture[118] on the same level as Napoleon, but in all other respects they are, or wish to be, very different from their elders. And yet, when I enquire what they hope to do in the future, their ardent reply is: 'politics'. One was educated in Paris (rue St Guillaume), the other in Zurich's Polytechnicum. Together they plan to found an agrarian party. 'The town-dwellers are riff-raff in comparison with the wonderful rural population.'

In the afternoon, I phone C., the director of *Le Nouvelliste*.[119]

'Mr C. is not available.'

'Where can I contact him?'

'In prison'.

He's been arrested for publishing a rather innocuous article on the obstacles preventing Mr Borno from making an official visit to the Dominican Republic. For once, this opposition-friendly journalist, whom the Americans regard as an enemy, must be grateful for the US presence in Haiti. For, were it not for that, he would have been taken long ago, stood up against the graveyard wall, and shot.

Immediately after it became an independent Republic, Haiti sent some unusual diplomats to Europe. One of them, Haiti's previous ambassador to France, on being re-appointed to his old diplomatic post, lost so much money playing cards that he was unable to pay his debt to his opponent. Instead, he offered to the latter the man who was with him and whom he identified as his slave. The lucky winner went off to examine his new acquisition:

'Show me your teeth and remove your clothes,' he ordered.

'What do you mean?'

'I mean that your master has sold you to me.'

---

118 Toussaint Louverture (1743-1803) played a pivotal part in the Haitian slave insurrection of 1791. His military and political role was instrumental in freeing Haiti (then called Saint-Domingue) from French rule and in paving the way for Haitian sovereignty. The Haitian Republic was established in 1804, a year after Toussaint Louverture's death in exile in the Jura Mountains in the snow-bound Fort de Joux, where he had been lured and imprisoned by the French.

119 Founded in 1898, *Le Nouvelliste* is Haiti's oldest daily newspaper.

'But sir, I'm not a slave', replied the other indignantly, 'I'm His Excellency, Haiti's ambassador to London.'

At table all the talk is of politics. The Haitians are first and foremost Latins rather than Blacks. So much so that it never even occurs to them that, in their struggle against American domination, they should connect with the American Blacks who vote Democrat or with the US Association for the Advancement of Colored People.[120] Nobody here reads, knows about or has even heard of *The Crisis*, *The Chicago Defender* or the other major press outlets for American people of colour. And yet, who better to understand and defend the Haitians than their American brothers?

DECEMBER 9TH

Apparently it's customary here in Haiti to rise at 4.30 a.m. The servant brings in the breakfast. She's not fat, but her muscled flesh is so heavy that she makes the whole timber house quake; as she passes by I can feel the floor tilt beneath my bed. At 6 a.m., the air is deliciously cool. '*The vast pure breath* of the trade wind' evoked by Lafcadio Hearn[121] can be felt blowing at this hour more than at any other time of day. The sky is such a tender green colour that it looks like beautiful, evenly tinted skin. On awakening, I can see the Haitian National Guard from my window. Dressed like Americans, they are doing a weapons drill on the 'battleground' or 'Champ de Mars' as it's called. All of a sudden I hear the great black 'Sammies' roar out in ferocious French: 'Wan Too Tree Foah'.

Once again I spend the entire day in the great deserted Seaside Inn. Once evening falls, the rats and mice, the lizards

---

120 The National Association for the Advancement of Colored People was founded by W.E.B. Du Bois and others in 1909 as a response to race-based discrimination in the USA.

121 This is a quote from the chapter 'La Grande Anse' in Lafcadio Hearn's *Two Years in the French West Indies*, Oxford: Signal Books, 2001 [New York: Harpers, 1890], p. 114. Hearn evokes, more precisely, 'the vast pure sweet breath of the wind' at Saint–Pierre.

and shrews turn out in force, along with the hysterical laughter of the parrots, who call me 'honey pie' in a most arrogant manner. They remind me of two Australian parakeets that I encountered in Singapore, in 1925.[122] Parakeets are the most sweet-talking birds of the entire parrot family, and this pair was posted at the front and the back door, respectively, of an address of ill-repute. The first roared 'This way! Come on in!' and the second, at the exit, 'Call the doctor!'

I've been invited to tea by the most worldly of Haitians, Mr L., general secretary to the minister of home affairs. On the walls, amongst the family photographs, I spot a picture of Maurice Rostand[123] and of the Rochefoucauld Cocéa family.[124] Outside, above the breadfruit tree, rages one of those tropical storms that make it seem like the sky has colic.

The drinks on offer here are extremely sweet: they're made from sugar syrup and rum. The punch is delicious and is served ice cold. We French have lost the habit of drinking punch, but it was much in favour in both England and France in the eighteenth century and at the beginning of the nineteenth too. In Haiti it's served from a glass pitcher, with a big block of ice in the middle and it's made with two bottles of champagne to half a litre of rum, half a litre of pineapple syrup, a quarter-litre of brandy, one whole pineapple, a little cinnamon and some slices of lime.

On August 9th 1777, the French king issued an edict forbidding Negroes and Mulattoes from entering the kingdom.

---

122 Morand had visited Singapore on the Asian voyage of 1925 that yielded *Rien que la terre* (1926). See pp. 7-8.

123 Maurice Rostand (1891-1968) was a noted novelist and poet and son of Edmond Rostand, author of *Cyrano de Bergerac*. See p. 72, note 85.

124 Alice Sophie Cocéa (1899-1970) was a Romanian-born French singer and film actress who married Count Stanislas de la Rochefoucauld, Duke of Bisaccia in 1926 (the writer Colette acted as their witness). The marriage ended in divorce in 1931 and the actress's second marriage was to a businessman who turned out to be a Nazi-sympathizer during the Occupation. She herself was arrested on that suspicion after the war.

One hundred and fifty years later the same law regulates US immigration.

I'm to pay a visit this evening to Dr O.. His hair is like one of those brooms that you find on ships, made of thousands of tails of rope. He specializes in voodoo studies and laughs like a parrot, without moving his face or his round eyes. Like all occultists, he boasts an erudition that is a curious mixture of convincing, scientifically-proven facts and absurd supernaturalism. All of this is presented in a supremely matter-of-fact manner even though the most eccentric of etymologies are marshalled as evidence. What struck me as particularly strange is the fact that, for Dr O., voodooism is the most perfectly rational (albeit magical) interpretation both of cosmology and of the study of the origins of our species. What's more, he sees this interpretation as being related to Egyptian tradition.

Initiates of the voodoo sect use the Hebrew language quite fluently. For them there are no Redskins or Yellowskins: they see only Whites and Blacks and predict that the world will end in a general fusion of the two races (this is my own pet theory too). In voodoo belief, the earth is part of a burning nebula of which only the sun now remains. This nebula has already propelled Saturn, Venus and all the constellations into outer space. The doctor also recounts a version of the flood story that is similar to the narrative of the Book of Genesis. Moreover, he attributes to that same adverse event the disappearance of Atlantis. This belief tallies, of course, with Bohemian lore, itself of Egyptian origin. It's interesting to note that the voodooists, just like the Hindoos, call the universal spirit by the name Hom or Om! Their ceremonies are held in secret and the doctor has confirmed that no Whites are ever seen there. True, Whites may be admitted to certain dances, but only if, when their mind is read, no dishonourable motives are uncovered. Even then, they are invited, not for their own benefit or pleasure, but rather because the presence of a white man is necessary in any festivities where the object of the ceremony is to celebrate the mystical union of Whites and Blacks. This is why, not daring to request the presence of Europeans, the Blacks often play the role of Whites by painting their own faces with white clay. At these ritual celebrations, there is always a medium present, along with two women. One of these, a pythoness, is in communication with the Higher Powers, and the other, a necromancer, is in charge of calling up the dead. There is also a particularly curious character that I've seen in photographs: a woman who is supposed to be the wife of Saturn (whose son is Satan). She is wearing men's clothes – a top hat and a black jacket over her white dress – and she's holding a skull, a scythe and a sledgehammer. The drums roll as all the assistants, who are dressed in white, get sprayed with the blood of the sacrificial victims: goats, chickens, and other animals. According to the good doctor, and to Father Moreux[125], the geodesic and cosmographical measurements that form the very basis of the science of proportions (standard metals and measurements), are all located inside the Great Pyramid of Egypt. Moreover, concealed beneath the Egyptian Sphinx lies the entrance to an inviolate tomb whose secrets are of the utmost significance for the explanation of the universe.[126]

The word 'fetish' comes from the Portuguese and is itself derived from the Latin word *factitus*, meaning the 'art of magic'.

---

125 Théophile Moreux, *La Science mystérieuse des Pharaons*, Paris: Librairie Octave Doin, 1923.

126 We read here the second of the only two footnotes in Morand's text. 'I have learned that the good doctor (Dr O.), who is clearly *the* authority on the matter, was interviewed at great length by W.B. Seabrook, the author of *The Magic Island*, such a great hit in New York. Indeed, that interview is referred to in the book. Seabrook spent a long time in Haiti: he plunged himself deep into the countryside, witnessing scenes of huge significance. He was thus able to report that, contrary to the rejection by both Americans and locals of the widespread presence of Voodoo, there are in Haiti alone thousands of Voodoo altars, hundreds of thousands in his view.' Seabrook (1884-1945) was an American explorer and occultist. His book was published in New York by Blue Ribbon Books in 1929, with an author's foreword dated September 1928.

CARIBBEAN WINTER

DECEMBER 10TH

French military history is forever rehashing stories of 'one against a hundred' or 'one against a thousand'. Our entire naval history revolves around that one heroic boat, which – having held out against the entire English Navy – ended up going under. In fact, however, sound strategy consists in being ten against one, when it counts.

And what of that disregard for sanitation that caused slaughters from which no lessons were ever learned? In Haiti, in 1802, yellow fever shrank Leclerc's army from twenty-five to eleven thousand men in three months and so we lost the island. And did we learn from this catastrophe? Did we realize we had to abandon the lowlands and fight back against epidemics? Not at all. In the province of Vera Cruz, during the Mexican war, fifty thousand Frenchmen died of yellow fever. In Tonkin province, it was the same story; and much later still, in Madagascar, our expeditionary forces were decimated once again by an epidemic. Conversely, in the colonial wars fought by the English, it is clear that, right from the eighteenth century onwards, their armies always set up camp in the highlands.

Today, yellow fever, which is still raging in Dakar, has disappeared from Brazil, Panama and Guatemala. And this is because the Americans are enforcing hygiene regulations: 'Is that a pot of water in your garden over there? Well, you're going to have to empty it because it attracts mosquitoes.' The next day, the health officer comes by and finds the pan still there. 'That's a twenty-dollar fine for you and the next time it will be three months in prison.' In Colón, as soon as a settler sees a mosquito, he must notify the authorities by telephone. A boy arrives at once with a net and the captured mosquito is sent directly by the relevant office to the laboratory where its place of origin is identified. That triggers a Public Health offensive with officials in masks and white gloves descending on the location like firemen.

DECEMBER 11TH

Lunch today in T. with the parish priest. He's from Brittany and has built the parochial house with his own hands. There are two bedrooms, one camp bed, several holy books, sundry tools including a drill, collections of seeds and a colonial helmet. Also, a motorbike with lots of spare springs because the roads are atrocious. In order to reach this place we've had to ford six rivers. We're joined for lunch by another man of the cloth from Flanders; he looks like a benefactor in one of the donor portraits from the so-called 'Primitive School' of Flemish painting. The parish priest shakes his cocktail maker as though it were the most natural thing in the world. Then he places the drinks on a tray and says the blessing above the glasses. Although he has been living alone here for years, overseeing a parish of some twenty-four thousand Blacks, he's full of good humour and vitality. Eating heartily, he tells me how he once had to give the last rites to a leper. Since the man's head and entire body looked like one big wound, it was hard for him to find a spot of flesh sufficiently intact to anoint.

Above our table, birds of prey are gliding, skating in wide circles across the open sky.

Our host recounts that he was once asked by a solicitor friend of his to witness the signature of a will in the countryside. The two of them arrived in the dying man's bedroom, which was already crowded with relatives. On the bed lay not somebody at death's door, but rather a corpse. A question and answer session began: 'To whom are you leaving the ten acres of *Grand Morne*[127]?' asked the closest relative. 'To Sami, isn't that right?' With that, the dead man twisted and turned in his bed, moving his arms and legs. 'There, you see, he's saying yes,' said one of the heirs, so the solicitor wrote down 'Ten acres of land for Sami.' And so on. Smelling a

---

127 *Grand morne* means big hill or mountain.

rat, the priest looked under the bed only to discover that a Negro who was hiding there was pulling on a string tied to the limbs of the corpse. Full of indignation, he was on the verge of refusing to sign the will. However, the solicitor told him that it was established practice in this region to resort to ventriloquism when a person dies intestate and that he would do better to play along with custom.

What Haiti brings to mind is Tortoise Island or the Bay of Thieves from Oexmelin's[128] tales. In other words, a past peopled by the pirates of Holland, France and England, all united in a shared hatred of the Spanish crown. One can readily imagine Raleigh, Hawkins and all the big Elizabethan sharks disporting themselves here – all those admirals with black beards adorning their ruffs like necklaces. And one can picture too the chests full of gold coins – Spanish dollars – and hear the proclamation of James I from Whitehall in 1608, describing the pirates in the following terms: 'lewd and ill-disposed persons accustomed to spoile and rapine ... such foul crimes, most hatefull to the King's minde and scandalous to his peaceable government'.

It's Sunday and out on the open road we pass men on horseback, seated without stirrups on saddles made of millet leaves. They are using a length of rope as reins and are wearing big straw hats, made of palm fronds. This is, in its purest state, the rural lifestyle that gives Haiti its charming, old-fashioned character.

This evening after dinner, I hear a dull drumbeat coming from the countryside. All over Haiti, in every village, people dance on Saturdays and Sundays right up to four o'clock in the morning. Leaving the main road, I enter a circle of beaten earth and move into the pitch-black shade of the palm trees.

---

128 Born around 1645 in Honfleur to an exiled French Protestant apothecary, Alexandre Olivier Exquemelin (also written Oexmelin) died in Harfleur around 1707. In 1678, he authored in Dutch an important study of seventeenth-century Caribbean piracy.

There I come upon a group of men playing bones on trestle tables beneath a thatched roof from which hangs a resin lamp. Further on, two seated men are beating drums with their palms. About twenty men and one woman are dancing a *martinique*. It's a dull, plodding, bestial dance; the male dancer gyrates on his own or in front of the woman, but without touching her. All of those present get caught up in the same convulsive movement, swaying their bellies in time. It's reminiscent of the dances of the Moyen-Chari region of Chad, the setting for the film, *La Croisière noire*.[129]

Love ivy or 'come-on ivy'[130] is a creeping plant much used in Haiti. It is soaked in water to produce an aphrodisiac drink. Fr R. tells me that his parishioners drink it to no great effect, but that's not what young T. says when I ask him if he's familiar with the beverage: 'I think so,' he tells me, 'and I wasn't able to sit down for two days afterwards.'

In Haiti, Martinican women have a reputation for beauty. They're accused of being attracted to one another, a vice that is very rare in the Antilles. Haiti, on the other hand, is a most moral place where there's no room for courtesans. The upper classes go in for the kind of sentimental liaisons depicted in novels from the end of the nineteenth century where courtship always ends up in a book of poems. The rest of the time love is just a bourgeois plaything, so to speak, and utterly insipid. There's no money in Haiti and very few foreign tourists, and this all makes for a narrow social atmosphere: an early-to-bed, gossipy and perfectly contented provincialism, where everybody is related to everybody else.

Caribbean Blacks are ashamed of their colour, certainly. But

---

129 Meaning 'Black Voyage', this was a film about a Citroën-sponsored expedition to Central Africa that took place between October 1924 and June 1925. Beyond its commercial inspiration, the project had considerable political and cultural resonance in France.

130 Morand gives the graphic Creole expression for tumescence: *liane-bandi*.

what humiliates them the most is their hair. 'You're so lucky to have such straight hair,' they're always saying, enviously. This inferiority complex, totally foreign to their African brethren, is especially obvious in the writing of the Caribbean half-caste, Maran.[131]

In Port-au-Prince there's a barber's shop called 'Five Minutes to Mulatto' because the Blacks all emerge from it with straight hair and powdered skin: transformed into Mulattoes, in other words.

It's in the wake of Romanticism that Haitians started writing verse in earnest: now all of them are at it. What happens when I stop in some village to buy petrol? Why, the owner rushes over to sing the praises of his book of French verse, published at his own expense by one of those obscure French vanity presses that have cornered this particular market. The collection boasts *rondeaux*, ballads and other archaic forms. My two young friends are the only ones to have ventured further than imitations of Samain.[132] At this rate, it will take Haiti until 1950 to get as far as imitating Valéry. The country as a whole is extremely 'right-wing' in its literary taste: witness the fact that nobody here has even heard of Mallarmé or Claudel.[133]

Having a book of poems under his belt gives a man a certain social status. It opens doors, especially onto a career in politics or the civil service. Yet, if he has penned several books of poetry, his status immediately plummets, because that means he has

---

131 René Maran, born to Guyanese parents in Martinique in 1887, was educated in France and worked in colonial administration in Africa, in the Oubangi–Chari region, now called the Central African Republic, before moving back to France as a journalist, dying there in 1960. In 1921, his novel *Batouala* was awarded the Prix Goncourt.

132 Albert Victor Samain (1858-1900) was a writer and Symbolist poet born into a Flemish family in Lille (northern France).

133 Stéphane Mallarmé (1842-1898), Paul Valéry (1871-1945) and Paul Claudel (1868-1955) were all distinguished and highly original (post-)Symbolist poets and writers, whose poetry was very influential for Modernist and Post-Modernist writing in French.

become a hack, a professional scribbler.

The most pernicious thing ever to befall Haitian poetry was Arvers'[134] famous sonnet. This poem is ubiquitous in Haiti: you'll find it printed on silk, adorning lace doilies and stamped on the bottom of soup-bowls.

DECEMBER 12TH

Haitian taste in painting provides the single biggest market for the French art exhibited in our official 'Salons'. And as for the interior decor of private houses, I might quote from a local novel the following description, which strikes me as spot on:

'The Xs' drawing room left one with an impression of incomparable beauty. Close by a Pleyel piano, draped in silk, stood a little bijou lacquered table; upon its marble top was placed an eighteenth-century lamp made of porcelain and mounted on bronze. At the back of the room a large rectangular table bore two bronze statuettes depicting strong- and supple-limbed Tunisian water-carriers... The white wall panels were hung with photographs in pink-lacquered frames. All of these objects, which here bespeak unheard-of luxury, had been purchased in Paris.'

In Cap-Haïtien, the oldest French town on the island, one still finds furniture dating from the colonial period. The revolutionary slaves held on to the furniture of their masters like so many relics. (Mr Lévy-Bruhl[135] has demonstrated the importance of a sense of belonging for the primitive mind and the way that familiar objects, the ones surrounding an individual

---

134 This sentimental love poem, 'Un secret' by Félix Arvers (1806-1850) was perhaps the most popular poem in French of the entire nineteenth century. It first appeared in 1833 in Arvers' collection *Mes heures perdues*.

135 Lucien Lévy-Bruhl (1857-1939) was a philosopher whose work in the pioneering fields of sociology and ethnology was concentrated on the exploration of the so-called 'primitive mind', which he contrasted with the logical or rational mind.

throughout his life, come to constitute an extension of that person's identity.) In Haiti, the most recent style to find favour was Louis Seize. Thus today, whenever provincial carpenters or cabinet-makers are commissioned to produce a wardrobe, they automatically follow the Louis Seize model.

It is not possible right now to get to Sans-Souci, the ruined stone fortress that King Christophe[136] had built for himself not far from Cap-Haïtien at the start of the nineteenth century. The road has recently subsided and is still blocked.

This morning we have lunch at eleven o'clock in R.'s plantation. It's a demesne as vast as the entire Canton of Geneva. The table is set in a barn amongst the fields of banana trees and sugar cane that stand out against the blue background of the mountains. The plantation manager, a former general who has retained nothing of the military save his spurs, dines with us. He's a decent old fellow, very black, with a grey moustache, all in all an excellent man, nobody's fool. We're served rum, a Pouilly white, a Moulin-à-Vent red and Clicquot champagne, all downed in the blazing heat and the ferocious glare of the noonday sun. It seems that the Negro, Paul Bourget[137], mentioned by Reboux in his book on the Antilles, exists in real life: he's head waiter here. When he's asked if he is related to the French writer of the same name, he replies: 'It's quite possible, for my long-departed father

---

136 Henry Christophe, a one-time slave, was one of Toussaint Louverture's lieutenants from 1793. After Toussaint was captured and exiled in France, Christophe continued to fight under General Dessalines. However, following the declaration of Haitian sovereignty in 1804, Dessalines was assassinated and Christophe was named as leader. He vacillated between despotic and democratic tendencies until hostilities broke out between him and his rival for power, General Pétion, who eventually defeated him in 1807. Pétion established himself in the South and Christophe moved north in 1807, proclaiming himself King Henry I in 1811. He built many palaces and fortresses and distributed the plantations amongst his soldiers. In 1820, having suffered a stroke, he took his own life and his kingdom became part of the Republic of Haiti the following year.

137 Paul Bourget (1852-1935) was a conservative novelist and critic.

was a great traveller.' There's a Paul Morand in Haiti too. He's a medical student. I'd quite like to meet my double, this black man who could be, for all I know, my second father.

Everybody knows how important names are for the Negroes. It's the one and only thing that they cannot resist receiving from us. And so one particular Negro from Cameroon, who had been orderly to a German officer to begin with and subsequently to a French officer, adopted the moniker Ludendorff-Foch.

There are so many egrets in the fields that all the quilts and pillows are stuffed with their feathers; the siestas enjoyed on the latter are called *cabichas*.

In the countryside, I've come across men dressed as women; I'm told that this is how contagious persons are identified. (Unfortunately the reverse is not the case.)

As though their own political conflict were not enough, the Haitians are delighted to adopt ours in addition. All the young men from here are loyal either to the king or else to the Reds. One of them said to me with some considerable pride: 'Did you know that I was involved in the de Harcourt business? Yes indeed, I got myself deported for hitting a police sergeant with a tankard (*sic*) on the Boulevard St Michel.'

When the Haitians say that they like us French, that just means that they hate the Americans. In the same way, the Filipinos, ever since the Spaniards were replaced by the Yankees, have suddenly discovered that they are, after all, in love with the former, who were the first to dominate them and whom they had so execrated in the past. The Americans, who have had only one constitution since 1776, are despised by the Haitians who – in the second half of the nineteenth century alone – can boast of the Constitutions of 1843, 1846, 1859, 1861, 1867, 1874, 1879 and 1888. All of these were, according to Texier[138], regeneration initiatives, in other words designed to restore to the nation the free exercise of the rights that had been trampled upon by the

---

138 Charles Texier, *Au pays des généraux: Haïti*, Paris: Calmann Lévy, 1891.

deposed tyrant.

DECEMBER 13TH

Lunch at the seaside. Some small oxen are moving forward through the mud, quite delighted to be drinking salt water. The same old pelican keeps running forward with his beak thrust out in front of him. He then dives down, beak first, into the water, and when he surfaces again the skin of his throat visibly swells out as he salivates and swallows his fish.

In Haiti people don't kill grass-snakes; it's a throwback to when they were totems.

I once wrongly claimed that the Negroes have never heard of the Charleston. But then I asked a young Black from Port-au-Prince if he knew the dance. 'Yes,' he replied, 'I learned it in Saint-Lunaire.[139] And when I returned to my parents' plantation last winter, I taught it to the country folk. Once I told them that it was a French dance, they all wanted to see what it was like.'

This evening I'm going back to the city. The air is so still that the car is full of vague stagnant smells. There's the stink of the tanneries, of animal carcasses and of incense; the most disgusting smell of all is of old tyres that have been burned in order to fend off evil spirits.

The most entertaining section of the local newspapers features legal notices like the following: 'I, the undersigned, hereby give notice to the Republic in general and to trade in particular that I am no longer responsible for the debts of Mistress Z., my spouse, whom I have repudiated for an act of adultery committed without my consent.'

DECEMBER 14TH

I hear complaints in Port-au-Prince about the Syrians. 'In the four or five years since Syrians have discovered Haiti, insurance

---

139 Saint-Lunaire is a coastal town in Brittany.

costs have quadrupled because they routinely over-insure their houses before setting fire to them.'

In black countries, as in any country where women stop taking exercise once they're no longer obliged to work for a living, only the commoners have lean bodies, perfectly rhythmic movements and an upright bearing. Conversely, bourgeois women run to fat and go pear shaped, developing huge behinds (a deformity called steatopygia).

As soon as night falls, Port-au-Prince is engulfed in a deep silence. People dine at half-past six and many are abed by half-past seven or eight o'clock. Where, oh where, is the riotous tropical nightlife of Saigon or Honolulu? 'Blame its absence on our poverty and on the exorbitant prices the Americans make us pay for their electricity.'

The Port-au-Prince bourgeoisie speaks neither the archaic French of Canada nor the local dialect that Hearn calls the 'beautiful childlike speech of French slaves'. Instead, they speak like books, for example: 'The waves unfurl over the beach like sheep's wool.' Their language reminds one of Barrès' description: 'The brains of children hijacked by the language of experts'. With few exceptions, Haitians have lost touch with living French, a language that is made and un-made in Paris. So, when I say to my driver: 'Keep an eye on my things,' he replies: 'I shall exercise over your luggage my alert and efficacious surveillance.' This isn't 'Baby French' at all; it's 'the French of Grandees'.

I often wondered where the expression *nègre marron*, meaning 'runaway slave', came from. I'm told that the word *marron* is derived from the Spanish *cimarron* meaning 'wild'. According to Mr Peytrand[140], the term *cimarron* itself comes from 'Symarron', the name of a tribe from somewhere near Panama, which took refuge in the forests after having rebelled against the Spaniards.

I've never heard people speak so much of Paris or France. Oh

---

140 Lucien Pierre Peytrand, *L'Esclavage aux Antilles françaises avant 1789*, Paris: Hachette, 1897.

to live in Paris: this is apparently what the entire world dreams of! The French imagine that it's because everyone loves them. But in fact, those outsiders for whom Paris is paradise detest France. The only thing that foreigners know about French history is the history of Paris. They know nothing of Saint Louis or Henry IV, because for them France is all about Paris: the taking of the Bastille, the Revolutionary calendar, the Commune, the Battle of the Marne, and so on. So even though the Greek colony in Paris is more Anglophile than Francophile, it would never occur to them to move to London, let alone to Athens. And this is why a man who was neutral in the Great War was overheard saying 'I can't wait for the Germans to win so that I can go back and have fun again in my beloved Paris.'

It must be said, however, that the love that Haitians have for France is sincere; they really do understand the country and are themselves French both in culture and in sensibility.

DECEMBER 15TH

Here I am aboard the German freight ship *Mira*, which is to depart at first light. It's torture to have to sleep on board a ship in port. Although there's not a breath of air, the portholes are closed against the coal dust and against burglary. Inside this iron hull, the temperature is white-hot after a day of double-strength sunshine, the glare having been reflected and amplified by the water. The merchandise is loaded all through the night, the darkness resounding with the din of pulleys, cranes and winches. In the morning we[141] learn that we won't be raising anchor until noon. After that, our departure is postponed from hour to hour. It's always like this on freight ships. Then finally, just as night is falling, we're off. Surrounded by a cargo of live chickens and turkeys bound for Jamaica for 'Christmas', we're the only passengers on board.

---

141 The slippage here from 'I' to 'we' reminds the informed reader that Morand is travelling with his wife, Hélène.

After having witnessed the spectacle of a minor collision between an American cargo boat and the Dutch ship that ran into it in the dusk, the ship pulls out of port, leaving behind the red glow of the beacon installed on the cathedral of Port-au-Prince. The captain of our vessel is an old sea dog who speaks Low-German, almost a form of Dutch. Although he spent five years in prison in England during the war, like all seamen, he respects England and detests America. It has to be said that the Americans are quite brutal in those ports where the dollar is king.

In a recent book, *The Antillean Agony*[142], which recounts his travels to the Caribbean islands in 1926-27, a brilliant Spanish writer of the new generation, Luis Araquistáin, claims that the pattern of decline and fall enacted in the Caribbean by all the colonial nations – with the single exception of Spain – is still ongoing thanks to the United States. Those other colonial powers Africanized the Caribbean, according to him, because instead of colonizing it directly, they did so indirectly by means of black manpower. Araquistáin needs to be reminded that, if the white nations resorted to black labour in the Caribbean, it was because the Spaniards had massacred the indigenous people to begin with. And it could also be argued that, physiologically, Blacks adapt to the Caribbean more readily than do Whites. The other salient point to be made is that once they struck rich, the Spaniards didn't stay around any longer in the region than did any of the other colonizers. During the reign of Philip II, the Spanish aristocracy didn't visit their mines in the New World any more often than the nobles of the court of Louis XVI visited their plantations in Haiti, which, at this time, were producing three-quarters of the world's sugar. In fact, the distribution of Caribbean land amongst the Spanish soldiers and the small-holder regime that resulted from that distribution barely survived Columbus. It was in reality the latifundaries who drew Mexico

---

142 Luis Araquistáin, *La agonía antillana: el imperialismo yanqui en el mar Caribe*. (*Impresiones de un viaje a Puerto Rico, Santo Domingo, Haiti y Cuba*), Espasa Calpe, USA, 1928.

away from Spain as early as 1821. Although Araquistáin's patriotic sentiment is entirely justified, he seems unable to face facts. The truth is that each century of human history has been marked by the successive take-offs of different white nations: the Portuguese in the fifteenth century; the Spanish in the sixteenth; the Dutch in the seventeenth, the English in the eighteenth; the French in the nineteenth, while the twentieth century belongs to the United States. Araquistáin himself admits that US imperialist rule is currently absolute in Porto Rico, partial in Cuba, based on a financial and legal mortgage-hold in the Dominican Republic, military in Haiti and that the USA is currently annexing Panama and threatening Nicaragua. As far as I'm concerned, the independence of these bastardized states – states of hybrid composition that have been stripped of their indigenous races – is a matter of supreme indifference. Their serial colonization is a historical truism.

The captain owns a ghastly mutt, which – according to himself – is a cross between a polar bear and a canary. Just the ticket for a ship sailing between the Baltic and the Caribbean.

Gobineau's theories seem quite sound to me on the whole. But having recognized that 'the fountain from which art springs lies hidden in the veins of the Blacks' and having evoked the 'beautiful crown that belongs on the misshapen head of the Negro', why does he then go on to claim that 'this fountain is foreign to civilizing instincts'?

War is the natural state of relations between isolated peoples. It is possible that those who mingle and mix will detest one another, but at least they won't come to blows. Today the only belligerent peoples are those who are cut off from others by their political regimes: namely, the Russians and the Italians.

DECEMBER 16TH

It's been a suffocating day, spent trying to flee the vertical sunshine flooding a cargo bridge too narrow to hold two armchairs. The air from the engine-room is like Vulcan's breath. The sides of the vessel are sweating, exuding a sort of marine resin, for the naval glue used in cold countries as a caulk or filler has started to melt in the heat.

The sixty-year-old German captain, ruined by inflation, is obliged, despite his age, to work until he dies in order that his family might eat.

To thank us for speaking German with him, he draws from his safe some wonderful Westphalian[143] sausages. Towards evening, we spot the steep walls of Jamaica and its south-west corner, Morant Point. At the sight of these white cliffs, we automatically try to make out the castle of Dover. Right now the sea is the faded violet shade of certain types of steel. The huge submarine craters in this bay can reach a depth of eight thousand metres.

DECEMBER 17TH

I awake at dawn, at 5.30 a.m. There's a medical inspection at Port-Royal during which the British Empire is represented by a half-caste. The inquisition goes like this: Is this your first visit here? How long are you staying? Are you coming here to grow bananas, or at least to visit banana plantations? etc, etc. It's a strange sensation for anybody familiar with old, start-of-the-century Free Trade England, to witness its determination to hold on to its colonial monopoly even more jealously than Spain at the time of the Armada, or than Restoration France.

Since our boat is a cargo ship with no passengers, we have to spend two hours waiting for customs, for the doctor and for vaccinations. The hotel where I'm staying in Kingston, the capital of Jamaica, is a proper 'Ye Olde English' tropical inn. It's almost empty because the Yanks, the island's main tourists, don't

---

143 Westphalia is a region in north-west Germany. It is today part of the *Land* or federal state of Nordrhein-Westfalie and counts about eight million inhabitants.

arrive until after Christmas. We leave the city at once for a grand tour, travelling in a poor car on poor roads (which we've heard being praised to the skies and which are indeed impressive in comparison with Haitian highways). During our three hundred-kilometre trip we climb twice up to twelve hundred metres before coming back down to sea-level on the other, northern side of the island. We pass through Spanish Town, Moneague, Port Maria, Annotto Bay and the hills of Saint Andrew. Not only do the counties of Jamaica have English names like Westmoreland, Manchester, Portland, but the houses have bow and sash windows, the Blacks wear gold-rimmed spectacles, and the whole island is studded with the Gothic architecture of Anglican churches. Castleton Park and the Botanic Gardens exude that coldness so characteristic of Victorian respectability across the entirety of the royal realm. The lawns are reminiscent of Kent and, instead of becoming anaemic in the Tropics, the cattle are continually rejuvenated by the imports of fresh blood stock. There is an admirable police force and decency rules the roost.

English hypocrisy, which in an individual might be seen as a vice, proves to be a magnificent virtue for society as a whole. It means that the ruling classes never show themselves to the lower orders in a degrading light and that the Whites never lose face in front of the natives. This is all made evident by the attitudes of coloured people towards different categories of Whites. The American lets himself down by letting a native see him get drunk. The Frenchman lowers himself by walking in the street weighed down with parcels, by making egalitarian pronouncements, by shaking everybody's hand, making love to native women or recognizing his bastards. As for the Englishman, he is hated but respected.

These rich over-winterers are strange people. They take to the high seas for twelve days in search of heat, but as soon as they reach it, they do all in their power to flee it for the cool of the highlands. At twelve hundred metres, one could be in Scotland. The Blue Mountains, to take one example, is a place of green landscapes, golf courses, hotels and winter woollies.

The Blacks are infinitely less attractive in Jamaica than in Martinique or even Haiti. But the natural landscape is immeasurably more beautiful here. There is, for one thing, the sheer abundance of rivers cascading down into the sea, so that water seems to well up everywhere. The eye is caught by ferns standing four or five metres high, by giant bamboos and by trees fastened to the earth by aerial roots that begin twenty feet above the soil and then form vertical screens of vegetation that anchor themselves in the earth thirty metres away. Above the frozen rapids of the Rio Cobre, hosts of palm-trees gather together and merge into single file.

In the north, the shoreline belongs to the big American fruit companies, such as Universal Fruit or the Atlantic Fruit Company. As far as the eye can see, there are copra palm plantations and banana fields. These extend right down to the beaches of soft sand, the treacherous rocky reefs and the rolling waves. The only places where the swell subsides are the little creeks with beached canoes where you'd love to go swimming if someone hadn't pointed out, on the surface of the water, the suspect wrinkles tracking the dorsal fins of sharks.

Jamaica shares the same history as all the other Caribbean islands. It too was discovered by Christopher Columbus and its Indians too were hunted down by the bloodhounds belonging to the Spaniards of Pedro de Esquimel.[144] A single year saw sixty thousand natives perish and in the space of eighty-six years, more than six hundred thousand Negroes were imported from

---

144 Pedro de Esquimel was an early sixteenth-century governor of Jamaica under the Spaniards. His immediate predecessors were Juan de Esquivel and Francisco de Garay. He was regarded by Las Casas as the most cruelly destructive of the early governors of Jamaica. See William James Gardner, *The History of Jamaica: From Its Discovery by Christopher Columbus to the Year 1872*, (1873), repr. London: Taylor and Francis, 197, p. 11.

Africa. Another unifying feature was the discord amongst the conquering nations. Columbus returned to Jamaica a sick man and the object of much jealousy on the part of the governors; his ships were taking in water and his crews were mutinous. At sixty-three and suffering from gout, he was kept prisoner for a year on the pretext that he was receiving medical treatment. He didn't leave Jamaica as much as flee it, returning at seventy to die in Seville. At that point the English seized Jamaica from the Spaniards. Around the time of the French Revolution, the island took in a great number of French colonists, survivors of the massacres in Saint-Domingue.[145] These refugees provided a precious injection of wealth and industriousness. Today, the English are delighted to see the advent of the North Americans, whose big fruit companies are a welcome source of prosperity. Capitalism can be seen here at its best: the natives are well paid and their standard of living is rising; clean accommodation is being built for them and every plantation has its own hospital.

The earthquake that wiped out Kingston in 1907 left no trace behind. On the heights, in Newcastle, far away from the epidemics, Scottish regiments wearing kilts and sporrans keep watch over the Caribbean Sea. The Panama Canal has increased the strategic, commercial and tourist value of the island a hundred fold. Sheltered as it is from the gusts of the *Norte* (the icy wind that batters Cuba and Florida), Jamaica doesn't know what winter is.

Spanish Town dates from the sixteenth century, as does its ill-fated grandeur: the governors' palaces are in ruins and the grass on the former square of the Residence is strewn with antique

---

145 The Haitian Revolution began in the most prosperous European slave colony of the Americas, then called Saint-Domingue, around 1791, and culminated in the establishment of the first Black Republic. The proclamation was signed in January 1804 and the victorious general Dessalines gave an order that all Whites remaining in Haiti should be killed. Reports that up to 5000 white men, women and children had been brutally massacred travelled far and influenced many in the Southern USA against the abolition of slavery.

iron canons, trophies from forgotten naval victories. Beyond it, the road follows the Rio Cobre through one of the most beautiful tropical landscapes imaginable: it looks like a palm grove or like a billionaire's winter glasshouse, but on an exponential scale. It has been turned into a magical botanical chaos by a host of climbing parasites – various vines and creepers, convolvulus, so-called 'Spanish Beard' and so on. It smells of vanilla and is much more beautiful than the Haitian forest. Thanks to the abundant rainfall, the greenery has exploded with all the violence of the vegetation of the Guianas or of the Congo, but minus their mortal danger. In Jamaica the land offers everything one could ever ask for: kola nut, cocoa, sugar, spices, vanilla, tea, mangoes. And above all else, bananas.

DECEMBER 18TH

Tomorrow we head for Santiago de Cuba on a wretched, hundred-ton schooner. And so it is that voyages commenced on transatlantic liners end up on rafts. The crew boasts just two Whites and, while the captain is an Englishman, he is barefoot. The Caribbean islands are so far apart that, although it would only take an hour to cover the distance in a plane, one often has to wait fifteen days to get from one island to another by boat.

I'm living the life of an American of leisure and this has a certain charm when it only lasts two days. What is entertaining about travel is that one is passing horizontally through a cross-section of lives that will continue to develop vertically until the point of death.

From North America to Malaysia I've been the guest of hundreds of different populations, each of which thought itself the centre of the world.

This morning I went to the Bournemouth Swimming Pool. It's nothing like Bournemouth in England, whose drizzle, rhododendrons and melancholic inertia are an artificial creation of the Gulf Stream, in its death throes in the northern fog. At ten o'clock in the morning the glare is already unbearable. That's because this yacht club, which is more American than English in style, is located on the shore, beside a blazing, motionless sea that bathes in a hazy, jelly-like light the steamers and yachts of the over-winterers and the monotonous succession of palm trees and banana trees, banana trees and palm trees. Anybody who wants to swim in the sea, though it's not the done thing here, will find that a barbed wire fence has been erected in the water to protect swimmers from the sharks.

English lawns are everywhere. An artificial beach, in a concrete setting, is patronized by sunbathing aficionados, who lie on expensively imported sand that shimmers like mica. Above them is the swimming pool where seawater is pumped in and changed four times a day. Very black Cuban millionaires with long eyelashes, along with some Englishmen from Belgravia and some refugees from Park Avenue, dive in for a dip. The pool looks like the site of an orderly shipwreck. Children are floating in inflated tyres and bunches of them are jumping into the water from a slide. The presidents of American trust funds sit astride life-size inflated ponies made of rubber, which buck and throw their rider when he spurs them on. The water is disfigured by a plethora of various types of trampoline, platform and bunting. The self-same kind of carry-on has been inflicted on the Lido by a similar type of clientele. Just as they laid waste to the Hawaiian beaches, they are now destroying the Adriatic coast. The men are ugly, twisting around like segments of mutilated eels. Everybody is wearing the chaste and uncomfortable two-piece bathing costumes that are mandatory in America. There are some very pretty women, blondes, but naturally blond, so no dark roots. They've got nice bodies and long legs and are alluring in spite of the seawater, which deepens wrinkles, hardens facial features and makes hair sticky. Two of them, real beauties, are frolicking together. One is sitting on the concrete with her legs in the water. Her companion is immersed, but is holding herself up, her arms encircling her friend's thighs, her head resting on the beloved's knees.

Around the first-floor gallery, some layabouts are drinking Jamaican rum on ice from glasses fringed with caster sugar. Its unique flavour is produced by a dead slow fermentation process. Vultures are circling high up in the sky. A phonograph is playing. At this very hour, workers in Europe are getting up and pupils in boarding schools are breaking the ice in their washbasins.

DECEMBER 19TH

Why do the Kingston taxis have the word 'Pleasure' written in capital letters on their car doors? Is it because taxis are the massage parlours of the English-speaking world?

In the morning, all the fighting cocks of Jamaica crow in unison at six o'clock. It's a veritable riot of song. I once made the crossing from Barcelona to the Balearic Islands on board the *Don Jaime II*. In the morning, daylight was announced by a thousand cocks in cages on the middle deck. But even they didn't make as much noise as these Jamaican birds.

The Myrtle Bank Hotel in Kingston was built by the Americans, in other words by the United Fruit Company.[146] It's a well-known fact that the English could learn a thing or two from the Americans about the construction and outfitting of luxury hotels. The Myrtle Bank has a beautiful sea-front swimming pool, edged with palm trees that grow wherever they can, bent over by the wind. It also has a surfaced walking trail with distances indicated in big white letters painted on the ground like on the decks of ferries, and a bar where they make 'chiroo cocktails'[147]

---

146 The United Fruit Company was an American corporation founded in 1899 that traded in tropical fruit, mainly bananas, grown in Central and South America. Its chief competitor was the Standard Fruit Company.

147 There is no trace of this type of cocktail in any records consulted.

(one third Italian vermouth, one third gin and the rest made up with fresh pineapple juice).

In America, life's delights are accessible right from the moment of birth. You don't see adult men and women gorging themselves on pleasures just because, now that they've grown ugly, old and worn, they've finally got the means to indulge themselves. As Claudel[148] recently observed: 'What strikes me about the United States is that people start off there by getting a house and then take the rest of their lives to pay for it. Whereas in Europe, we have to work until we drop before we can afford to own a house.' It's only natural to have a house before starting a family. Here in Europe, young men are cut off from life by a mixture of interminable studies and exams and impecuniousness.

When my father was asked about my future, his favourite response was: 'What do I want to make of my son? A happy man.'

One of the surest signs of a great epoch is power in the hands of youth. Think of the Italian Renaissance with its youthful popes and 'great men', or of the French and American Revolutions with their generals aged twenty-four. Elderly leaders are the only ones whose errors have been irredeemable. The lesson that the Soviets learned from the USA was to give youth its chance and this is why they are so often backed by the young.

DECEMBER 20TH

Although outside the night is calm, our boat is pitching around like an old drunk walking home. I awake at 6 a.m. The water looks like shot satin. It makes me think of the fairy tale dress that was to be the colour of the sky.[149] At night, the water is asleep, its

---

148 Paul Claudel (1868-1965) was a Catholic poet, dramatist and diplomat and the younger brother of the sculptress Camille Claudel. Morand met Claudel in Saigon on his visit to Asia in 1925.

149 *Peau d'âne* is the title of a French fairytale in which a princess makes a wish for three different dresses: one the colour of the sky, the next the colour of the sun and the third the colour of the moon.

surface flat and smooth, but in the daytime it becomes crumpled again. It's full of flying fish that are as white as flour and as rigid as the metal fish advertising fishing-tackle on shop signs. They are leaping towards the sun, which has already rolled itself into a ball. As for us, we've already reached the southernmost tip of the island of Cuba.

Gide[150] never really brought me to the Black Sabbath. Or, as Massis[151] would put it, he never inspired satanic desires. Quite to the contrary, he gave me a healthy taste for early mornings, for happily starting work at dawn and for reading as a cure for bad humour.

The so-called twilight of the white nations is much talked about today though nothing is said about its cause. Yet, as early as the mid-nineteenth century, Gobineau ascribed it to the ravages of the egalitarianism propagated by the French Revolution. 'Since Whites had been separated by cosmic catastrophe from their counterparts of the two other species (yellow and black), they had no reason early on to imagine that any other type of human existed. Far from being shaken by the first sighting of yellow- or black-skinned men, this discovery merely confirmed their way of thinking. The Whites could not credit that they were looking at their equals when they beheld these hideous creatures, noting instead their nasty bestiality and their claim to the name "sons of apes"... etc.'.

Not long after Gobineau[152] wrote those lines, along came a

---

150 André Gide came from a family of Huguenots, late converts to Catholicism. He was awarded the Nobel Prize for Literature in 1947 and is known not just for his literary work but also for his open defence of pederasty, his anticolonial writings (especially in his work on the Congo) and his complete repudiation, following a trip to the Soviet Union, of a brief flirtation with Communism.

151 Henri Massis (1886-1970) was a writer, a critic and a conservative Catholic convert. He wrote on Gide in *Jugements II* (1924). Despite his collaboration with the Vichy government, he was an outspoken opponent of Nazism.

152 Gobineau. See p. 57, note 69.

White who himself laid claim to the name 'son of apes', namely Darwin, himself heir to Rousseau….

We arrive at eleven o'clock in Santiago de Cuba. We must wait two hours while Customs finishes his lunch, while Health and Hygiene finishes his siesta and until Immigration has finished smoking his cigar, and *Dios sabe*[153], the cigars smoked here are big and fat! At three o'clock we finally step onto dry land. There's no way of getting to Havana by road and no train until the following day. The afternoon is over by the time we finally get through customs and have our luggage registered.

We spend the evening in Santiago. All we've had to eat since Jamaica is some bread and even then we had to share it with a young Scot who, like us, couldn't stomach the food served on board. Here we're dining on delicious crabs with hot peppers and Havana pineapples, the best in the whole world, sweet and juicy. The Cuban men smell of French perfume and of cigars that we'd love to be smoking ourselves. On the cathedral square, everything is very Spanish: the big clubs, the Venus Hotel, the cathedral itself. The electric street lighting reveals a bevy of ravishingly beautiful girls, some of them Indian Mestizos, the rest of pure Spanish extraction, supple and blooming. It's obvious that they've spent the entire day sleeping and then getting ready for this outing. The most elegant are known here as the 'Houbigant girls'.[154] Big American cars, full of idle men, are cruising aimlessly around the cathedral which, like a medieval church or like American hotels, shelters shops and stalls at its feet. There are Christmas lottery tickets on sale. The heat is suffocating but the newspapers are forecasting temperatures of minus twelve in London and minus five in Paris. The shop windows are displaying cotton Santa Clauses in boater hats and there are endless acres of American shoes on display. As soon as people have them on their feet they go off to have

---

153 Spanish for 'God knows'.
154 Houbigant is a perfume brand founded in 1775 by Jean-François Houbigant, the preferred perfumer of Marie-Antoinette.

them shone (eighteen francs per shoeshine). Not that anybody ever really walks in them. Arabs, Hispanics and Orientals all love their feet and also their boots, more especially their daintiness and polish. The foot is a sexual symbol, especially for the Chinese, who lose all self-control at the sight of a naked foot.

A Cuban lady comes into the hotel with a dog like mine. I compliment her on it. 'Is it a gentleman?', I ask her in English, meaning what cannot be said directly in a more polite way (i.e. 'is it male?'). The lady doesn't quite understand my meaning. 'Sometimes,' she replies with a smile.

There are a lot of Negroes around. Negro officers. And mestizo women with reddish skin, wearing pink dresses and boasting straightened hair: real beauties. Araquistáin[155] had his book banned by the island authorities because he stated in it that that Negro blood is very widespread in Cuba.

The cars are still cruising round this square of thirty square metres. I count one hundred, maybe one hundred and fifty circuits. These are enormous vehicles with all imaginable accessories, including portside and starboard lights. At the wheel sit Negro chauffeurs in gold-striped uniforms. In the back seats, large ladies fan themselves, parting their damp thighs to let in some air.

Keyserling[156] is recently quoted in an Associated Press interview as saying that 'he was able to judge entire nations intuitively by deduction; all he had to do was to look at how five individuals act, speak and work, to be able to pass judgement on a whole people.'

DECEMBER 21ST

---

155 Araquistáin, see note 122.
156 Count Hermann von Keyserling was a German philosopher (1880-1945) and social Darwinist. He travelled widely in India, China, Japan and the Americas and wrote psychoanalytical studies on Europe, America and South America.

CARIBBEAN WINTER

I awake for the last time to a morning sky the colour of a turtle-dove's breast. At ten o'clock, the (American) train that crosses the length of Cuba is going to take us non-stop – over twenty-two hours and twelve hundred kilometres – to the opposite edge of the island, an island shaped, as the Spaniards put it, like a bird's tongue.

The landscape will remain tropical for a while, speckled with Negro cabins boasting just one door and just one window. The sugar fields, criss-crossed by lanes, stretch out as far as the eye can see. Towards evening, the air cools and the landscape flattens out. On the savannahs, the further one moves away from the Tropics, the bigger the cattle become and the plumper and more prepossessing they seem. Conversely and simultaneously, the palm trees become ever sparser and skinnier to the point of resembling nothing so much as flimsy feather dusters. The trails – for there are no roads worthy of the name – peter out at strange railway stations that are surrounded by Chinese-run bars and stores. Saddles and saddle packs litter the ground, especially on the station platforms. The Cuban cane is cut by Haitian Negroes and crushed by Spanish emigrants; the foremen are Cubans, the boilermen Poles and the mechanics Yankees. The entire Far West, which only lives on now in films, is still very much alive and kicking here. When night falls, a dreadful chill descends: it's only thirteen degrees Fahrenheit and the newspapers are forecasting zero temperatures in Florida. As I'm the only one wearing white clothes, I spend the night wrapped in newspapers. Luckily, there are several layers of protection because the newspaper in question is Sunday's *New York Times*.

DECEMBER 22ND

This morning, I'm back in Havana, eleven months[157] after I was last here. Z. and Y., two Cuban literati, are coming to see me.

---

157 On the chronology of Morand's travels, see above, pp. 9-11.

They have just been released from a prison term for a press-related felony. Z. is a Communist and is very proud of his four-year-old son who is already throwing stones at the police. And yet he hasn't dared to tell the child that he has been in prison; instead he has given him to understand that he has been at the office. 'Well, if the office really belongs to you, then you should try to get out of it from time to time,' was all the kid said. Z. has such a taste for subversion that, even though he's a pure-bred White, he passes himself off as a Negro.

Winter is upon us! Yet, in the constant summer of the Tropics you don't notice time passing. Perhaps it's the rhythm of the changing seasons that makes us Northerners hurry about so much.

X., a stylistic perfectionist, is facing posterity with no excess baggage and that's how he hopes to endure. Z., on the other hand, currently has a hundred thousand readers and couldn't care less about surviving his own death. The latter is read by the many, the former will be re-read by a handful. One readership extends into time, the other across space.

DECEMBER 23RD

According to V. de Laforge[158], all that would need to happen for Europe to return to the age of the reindeer – its natural climate – would be the building of a dyke from Key West to Havana. The Gulf Stream would then go off to moisten the coast of Morocco and France would find itself in the same boat as Labrador.

At least I'll be able to say that I was perfectly conscious of enjoying a world in its death throes. I was fully aware that I was seeing the last truly beautiful countries and receiving the final

---

158 There are no records of any climatological study by a V. de Laforge. Dominique Lanni, the editor of Morand's manuscript notes for *Hiver caraïbe* suggests that Morand may have been thinking of a V. de Lapouge (1854-1936), who was, however, an anthropologist rather than a geographer or climatologist. Vacher de Lapouge's best-known work is *Race et milieu social: essais d'anthroposociologie* (1909).

salutes to be proffered by still-respectful races. As a White, I'm travelling through the yellow and black worlds like an aristocrat receiving the homage of the peasants at the end of the eighteenth century. Although he's perfectly aware that none of it can last, he finds that at the start of July 1789 it's good to be alive…

Oh soft-bellied Havana, indolent Creole that you are, where have all your planters gone? Where are the old 'Isabella Age' settlers featured on the inside of cigar-boxes against a background of palm-trees, dressed in 'nankin' trousers, sporting double-beards and girded with gold medals? Surely for those who come to you from America on the trains introduced just this year (which do Havana-New York in forty-seven hours), the USA must be hell on earth. How else could they mistake you for that oasis of sultry repose that you indeed once were, but no longer are?

Havana is rich but brittle. Each polished surface is clean as a whistle. The entire place has been covered in concrete and is now devoid of shade and trees. All political and military disorder has been banished, along with that glut of cars and cash, that Latin anarchy that one finds oneself missing when it's gone forever, ripped asunder by American automobiles and screaming nickels. Even its Negro neighbourhoods and its Chinese quarter no longer afford a refuge to romantics. In Cuba the very air that people breathe is regulated by the share-price of sugar: its post-war fluctuations – rising from two to thirty cents after the war, only to fall again to three – can bring ruin or wealth with the speed of a cyclone. Sugar is behind all this extravagance, all this appalling luxury, which is largely a matter of vanity. Sugar is what pays for the sweet boxes bestowed upon courtesans, for the private villas masquerading as meringues, the Tudor mansions imitating American design, the small Trianons made of butter and the mountains of Italianate snacks and sweets. Since these excesses are rarely moderated by good taste, not only is the entire city made of marble, but all that marble comes from Italy. The new roads are made of granite and the ceilings of one Rhineland-style castle are decorated in mother-of-pearl. The same level of aesthetic attention is lavished on the Cubans' final dwelling-places. As I drove at speed through the Columbus cemetery, it was clear that every corpse has a marble villa, his own perpetual chalet, with stained-glass windows and ceramic gargoyles, a sort of funerary Viroflay.[159] The new hospital boasts sixty-five separate buildings, each one as big as an entire French hospital. In each of these buildings, a different type of illness is treated. Presumably, should you present with one of those serious types of leprosy from Central Asia, they'll have to put you in a sixty-sixth building which will be specially erected for you overnight. In Cuba, people count in millions of dollars. What couldn't one do with so much money? It has to be said that the most recent construction shows better taste. The influence of our Universal Exhibition of Design is starting to make itself felt. For example, the exquisite glazing of Lalique[160] is starting to adorn several residences and a Spanish and Jesuit renaissance is spurring on local art. In fact, some young Cuban artists, after their detour through Montparnasse, are now finding supremely apt inspiration in the Negro folklore and craftwork of the Caribbean.

Although it's true to say that the United States is all over Cuba like a rash – it has, after all, taken over farming and industry, including the sugar and tobacco industries and tourism too – it must be conceded that Cuba has taken its revenge. In this tropical Monte-Carlo, all the outlawed games

---

159 Viroflay is located about three kilometres from the palace of Versailles. Before 1932, when the Sully Vauban art deco residence was built, it was of no exceptional architectural interest. It is possible that Morand is referring here to Versailles or even that he confused Viroflay with Vézelay, home to an eleventh-century, Romanesque basilica that is a famous UNESCO world heritage site.

160 Lalique is a French company manufacturing high-end, luxury glassware. It was founded by René Lalique in Paris in 1887. The glassworks factory located in Alsace and founded in 1921 still manufactures the signature Lalique hand-blown glass vases.

are played, right into the morning. There are more than fifty all-night restaurants and four thousand bars and cafés in a city that counts no more than half a million people. Forty-five days are set aside each year for carnival, and every Sunday the whole town dresses up. It boasts the most beautiful golf course and a yacht club devoid of yachts. It goes without saying, moreover, that all the alcohol in the world, every drink – from Siberia to Australia – that has ever been thought up, fermented and bottled, is available here. On the 'patio' of the Hotel Sevilla, at cocktail time, in its Spanish-style inner courtyard, lined in porcelain and Granada tiles and decorated with tropical ferns and cages of Caribbean birds even noisier than American women, more is drunk in the hour between noon and one o'clock than in all of France put together. There is such a surfeit of beauty here that the courtyards are sinking beneath its weight. Everywhere you go, mouths are moving, eyes are sliding, laughter is erupting. The atmosphere is full of runs of good luck, random love affairs, furtive assignations, broken engagements, simmering divorces, inebriation, frivolity, gossip and scandal as well as blackmail. And yet the whole display is overlaid with that feeling of shame that the Anglo-Saxons can never quite shake off, especially when they are taking their pleasure in full view. Everything calms down at siesta time and only starts up again in the evening, after a day spent in the big Spanish-American country clubs in the suburbs. Dinner is served on the roof, where the darkness – one of the luxuries of the Tropics – is cancelled by the constellations of commercial lights. The type of tourist found in Cuba leaves, it must be said, a lot to be desired. The resorts abound, Hollywood-style, in music-hall stars, whiskey buccaneers, pirates and overly-blond typists dressed in stockings and suspenders, out on the town with their boss. The more sophisticated elements of American society go to Florida or the Cap d'Ail.[161] As for the higher-

---

161 This is a beach resort on the French Riviera near Monaco.

class Cubans, they are mostly holed up and invisible, except on gala occasions or Sunday-best days at the Country Club.

As soon as one can see past the flood of American merchandise, it's clear that goods from France are not just available here but are available in great supply: perfume, silk, wine, books, etc. For, the more the Yankee grip tightens on Cuba, the more the Cubans try to strengthen their links with Europe and more especially with France. So, when they're asked 'Why not New York?', their reply is, over and over again, 'And what about Paris?'

A number of Cuban intellectuals are Bolsheviks. They proudly display the enamel badge in their buttonholes and tell me that they are affiliated to the Kuomintang party and are networking with the Chinese in Cuba – especially the ones that frequent the Cantonese Club, for example – all of whom are revolutionaries (from Macao[162] and the south). But after a few minutes of conversation I can see that they have little or no interest in the Russian Movement or the Third International. Here, as in China, Bolshevism is just another face of protest nationalism and patriotism; it's just another way for Cuba's intellectual youth to react against the United States. Today, people are Bolsheviks in the same way that they used to be Freemasons, Republicans or *Carbonari*.[163] Such is the strange fate of Lenin's impossible doctrine: like so many religions, the further it spreads, the more absolute its loss of meaning and direction.

Tomorrow, the big CGT liner with its black and red chimneys will have left the harbour of Havana, a port guarded by the *morro*, that old Spanish fort so badly damaged by the terrible

---

162 Macao is a former Portuguese colony, now an autonomous region, located on the south coast of the People's Republic of China and just across the Pearl River delta opposite Hong Kong.

163 The term *Carbonari* (meaning 'charcoal makers') refers to an Italian network of secret societies, revolutionary in inspiration. It operated in the first decades of the nineteenth century and its liberal and patriotic ideology paved the way for the *Risorgimento* movement and ultimately for Italian unification.

cyclone of January 20th, 1926. After three days at sea we will reach Veracruz and that region of America known as Mexico, which all of four centuries ago loomed up before Cortés[164] thanks to a random storm. It's farewell, then, to this harbour, where the white, two- or three-mast Caribbean schooners lie slumbering. They are loaded with tobacco leaves, whose fermented, ammonia smell is so strong that the crew suck lemons as they labour.

For two days now, the ship has been churning up the Gulf of Mexico. We are floating on top of the world's boiler-house, the Gulf Stream, passing above the hidden reefs that litter the marine chart like fly droppings. Finally, one morning, the only breeze blowing on board is the one made by the fans. I leap out of bed to find that, beneath my feet, the liner is no longer this supple, spongy body sitting on a soft, sprung base; instead, it has hardened all of a sudden into a building set in concrete. Through the porthole, everything is blue. Then I see a fortress and three astonishingly tall palm trees. The landscape is so devoid of hope that it brings to mind Devil's Island or one of those haunts close to the Bahamas that the English pirates used as a base for sharing out the gold booty from the treasure chests. This is Veracruz, Mexico's foremost port; Veracruz, base-camp of the Spanish galleons; Veracruz, occupied by us French on two separate occasions in the nineteenth century.

Veracruz sends out a welcome party to meet us, so to speak. Alighting passengers are passed from one syndicate to another; from the porters' office to the taxi drivers' bureau, then from the beggars' union to the shoeshine office. The state of Veracruz and the city too have a very advanced administration regime: in other words, the whole show is close to falling apart; rents

---

164 The name Hernán Cortés (1485-1547) will always be associated with the conquest and destruction of the Aztecs. Cortés belonged to the first wave of *conquistadores* and his career began in present-day Haiti (Hispaniola) and in Cuba, before his expeditions to the Continent. Like Columbus, he died in Spain, embittered.

are not being paid and on the doors the red stars marked 'TRU' (Tenants Revolutionary Union) are reminiscent of Moscow. The mayor, another fellow traveller, is a fisherman by trade. Veracruz is not Mexico, however. From afar, the central government, although itself very left-wing, disapproves of these fashionable leanings, and represses them as best it can.

While waiting for the Mexican Railway to ring the bell signalling the departure of my train to Mexico City, I go for a stroll on the palm tree-lined promenade or *Paseo de los cocos*, a pleasant walk that winds up in a cemetery marked 'general'. There I rediscover the suffocating heat and clammy humidity of the Tropics with a joy proportionate to my knowledge that they are not going to last. After a few metres of surfaced pavement – the last reminder of the six-month American occupation in 1914 when President Huerta was in power – the old Spanish road takes over. It's punctuated with gaping chasms in which the municipal intestines of the sewers are clearly visible.

I arrive at the sea shore. Behind me, above the pink houses with their pockmarked verandas, clouds of domestic vultures – black *zopilotes* – hover like flakes of charred paper above a fire in the hearth. The huts are made of corrugated metal – the global architecture of tomorrow – and their inhabitants walk past me bearing on their heads those quintessential American vessels – square petrol cans full of water. By now my car is driving on the beach past cinemas that have subsided under the force of tropical cyclones and past the carcasses of ship-wrecked cargo ships or abandoned trawlers with their holds protruding from the waves. This is the real melancholy of today's world and it replaces the ruins that people came in search of to the Roman countryside a hundred years ago. Rails emerge from the water, showing that, long ago, there used to be public baths here. The barbed wire surrounding them was designed to provide an illusory protective barrier against the six sets of teeth of the sharks roaming the port. Finally, to complete and further soften the picture, the

Island of Sacrifices sits on the horizon. This is where the Indians, prior to Cortés, used to execute their victims. The latter were, however, less numerous than the six thousand Frenchmen who are sleeping their final slumber there on the orders of Napoleon III.

On the station platform stand some former convicts, freshly released from the fort of San Juan de Ulúa. They are selling their handiwork, fashioned from coconut shells. I'm waiting for the most opportune time to climb the mountain; it's an ascent through the three belts – hot, temperate and cold – leading up to the capital, each zone boasting its own city: Veracruz, Orizaba and Mexico. These three terraces are spread out over two thousand metres of altitude, extending right up to the top plateau. Cortés, who was attracted by the stories of the Indians and by the call of Aztec treasure, took six months to haul himself up there despite the friendly reception from the locals. The ascent made by our own French *zouaves*[165] was scarcely less of a challenge in a land that boasted no more highways then than it does today.

Thanks to the English railroad, I myself begin the climb in a comfortable Pullman[166], travelling through one of the most beautiful landscapes in the world, for which no tourist poster had adequately prepared me. The train is guarded by Mexican soldiers, with features and uniforms so Mongol in appearance that I feel I'm in China. Meanwhile, on the roof of the carriage, the lookout, who has to lie down flat when the train enters a tunnel, keeps watch over the ever-endangered track, standing upright, as though he were on top of a fortress.

In twelve hours time we'll be in Mexico City. First, though,

---

165 The *Zouaves* were an elite French regiment of light infantry intended originally (around 1830) to be recruited from Berber fighters, from Algeria mainly. However the regiment eventually included more Europeans and black Africans than Berbers. Morand is referring here to the 1861-67 Franco-Mexican war.

166 An extremely comfortable, luxurious railway carriage, usually a sleeping car.

we spend two hours rolling through a coastal desert of sandy dunes spotted here and there by dwarf palm trees, before the train starts charging towards the steep mountain slopes. It's at this point that the shamelessly luxuriant vegetation takes over: coffee trees, sugar cane, banana trees, all growing in separate zones as clearly demarcated as the various sections of a Colonial Exhibition. The fruits are all swollen to bursting-point. Crossing wooden bridges we pass over ravines and blue valleys that lie in the shade all day long, with waterfalls embroidering their slopes like lace collars. The resinous smell of the highlands is already merging with the steamy humidity of the coast. Heat and cold meet without blending. Instead, they engage in border combat. Snow eagles swoop down on parrots or on tropical egrets and the eye can take in both conifers and palm trees in a single sweep of the horizon. We are pulled along by two groaning locomotives, beautiful engines that bear the enchanting name of 'Fairlie'. After we have passed by the highest waterfall, at Atoyac, we notice that the trees, all entwined in creepers, are giving in to the climate. We are starting to emerge from the tunnels covered in a dusting of frost. This is the realm of forced banana and strawberries, these Mexican varieties that can be eaten all year round. The banana farms are submerged in a sea of giant banana leaves and pink blossom. The first time we see banana plants in the midst of an infinitely extensive tangle of vegetation, we're amazed to find that the bananas grow with their tips pointing not downwards, but upwards.

These wide-open volcanic valleys earn the description 'tragic' conferred on them by geographers. They resemble subsidence graves. Where is our own unique French oak tree in the sixty-five American species of oak? Since my eyesight is no use at all here, my memory tries to penetrate this tropical confusion. Where have I already come across a natural world like this Mexican one? Where have I already seen these wide tongues of twisted zinc, these ferns treated leaf by leaf with a primitive attention to detail? I'm struggling to place these symphonies of green, from yellow-green to vert-de-gris. All of a sudden it dawns on me: I know them from the work of Le Douanier Rousseau. Before becoming a customs official, the great painter took part, as we know, as a skirmisher[167] in the expedition to Mexico. From this chaotic landscape he brought back those bright hallucinations so beloved of the *concierges* of Montrouge[168] but which also went on to seduce the art dealers of the Rue La Boétie.[169] Yes, the only things missing from this natural world are the reclining grey Negro, the lions sporting manes that look like they've been curled with a hot tongs, the French tricolour and the clumsy signature of Rousseau himself, the nineteenth century's very own Cosimo Tura.[170]

We've entered a temperate zone now. There are fewer and fewer tunnels as, from now on, we circumvent the mountains, passing over horseshoe bridges. Night is falling. Here's Córdoba and there's Orizaba with its rococo church. On the latter's white facade the shadows of the palms are tracing huge dark shapes. Its steeple, full of punched-out eyelet openings, reveals a stairway that unfolds like a poem written on the spirals of a fairground kazoo. Also visible are the big breweries and the huge Mexican cotton factories owned by 'Barcellonettas', who are Frenchmen hailing from the Lower Alps. The city of Orizaba is situated half way up the mountains, between the sea and Mexico City. This is where the lowland planters rest up during the summer

---

167 The regiment of *Voltigeurs* (literally 'vaulters') was founded by Napoleon I in 1804. This was an elite regiment of skirmishers or outfielder infantry. It appears that the story of Le Douanier Rousseau's involvement in the Mexican campaign is apocryphal.

168 Montrouge is one of Paris's south-western suburbs, beside the 14th *arrondissement*. Le Douanier Rousseau (1844-1910) was associated with it.

169 This street, in the chic 8th *arrondissement* of Paris, is known for its art galleries and art dealerships.

170 Cosimo Tura (1430-95) was an Italian painter, known for his highly decorative style. He is said to have founded the Ferrara school.

months and where the highlanders come when their hearts are worn out by the altitude. The Church of San Miguel is partly hidden by the palm trees and the mountain peak of Orizaba is so high at almost six thousand metres altitude that it's invisible in the mist, thus accentuating the darkness and hiding even the brightest stars. Behind the green curtains of the railway carriage, the bracing air beckons one to sleep.

At dawn we awake on the plateau. The sun has already risen. Can it really have been only yesterday that we were sweltering in the foetid heat upon the sizzling soil of Veracruz, near an oozing coast with alligators and sea turtles slumbering in its saline swamps? This dry, brown plain, spotted with the aloe plants that yield *pulque*, the national drink, reminds me of Morocco and its sister landscape of Castile. What an amazing light! Limpid and harsh, mystical and arid. You would think that no insect, no larva, none of nature's low-lifes could possibly thrive in it and that it would render impossible the slightest decomposition. Distant space is spread out before our eyes in an immense, lunar circle. The mountains are clothed in a rigid flat coat of lava and each noise, each separate sound, reaches the ear with a strange distinctness and an inviolable beauty. Large puddles of salt and saltpetre reveal the former site of the lake of Texcoco, which has long dried up. This is the spot where the Aztecs built their city, the lake where Cortés halted. One of the many remarkable aspects of his expedition was that, no sooner had he reached this altitude, than he was forced to abandon his Andalusian horse and to start building, at more than two thousand metres, a fleet of boats. There was no other way for him to reach and to take the mysterious city on the far side of the lake.

The church of Our Lady of Guadalupe is a place of national pilgrimage. It's a pink citadel surrounded by toasted cypress trees and boasting bouquets of ex-votos like bunches of bananas. It proclaims that we have reached the gateway to Mexico City.

The eagle and the snake: no, this is not a fable. Or, if it is, it's a fable told to explain the tricolour background of the Mexican flag.

The sight of an eagle devouring a snake seemed to the Aztecs to be such a favourable portent that it convinced these migrants from the north to settle in this spot and found here what would become Mexico City. From the heights of the Acropolis of Chapultepec that towers over the city, it's difficult to imagine the lake where the Aztecs built Tenochtitlan in 1376. It must have looked like Venice or Bangkok with its floating islands and gardens, which live on today as a faint memory in the floating gardens of Xochimilco. On these same canals, in these same flooded streets, the Indians paddled their flower-strewn canoes. On these very heights, long before the reigns of President Calles and Emperor Maximilian, Montezuma II had established his summer residence, his harem, his baths, his aviaries and his hunting grounds. It was a place of languishing decadence and decomposition, but the civilization that was about to collapse when Cortés arrived on the scene had known heroic times and had been preceded by other, stranger civilizations that we are only beginning to glimpse today: savage, hermetic cultures, invisibly but incontrovertibly linked to Asia.

On this Sunday morning, between noon and two in the afternoon, Chapultepec is quite simply Mexico's Bois de Boulogne. Here before lunchtime, among *ahuhuetes*[171] and eucalyptus trees as twisted as *guimauves*[172], the Packards and Buicks belonging to rich Mexicans crawl along in a line, bumper to bumper. The Hispanic custom of the *paseo* has been inherited by all of Latin America. After mass or after the bullfight, people flock to this sedate parade of vanity and *ennui*, like the *paseo* down the Recoletos boulevard in Madrid or in Havana. The dearth of surfaced roads in the Caribbean does not prevent

---

171 The *ahuhuete* is a species of evergreen tree native to Mexico.
172 *Guimauves* are elongated French sweets made of multi-coloured strings of marshmallow in pastel shades, twisted or plaited together.

these processions of the indolent rich in their Rolls Royces, Hispanos and Voisins, all fitted with eight- to twelve-cylinder engines, with megaphones instead of silencers attached to all the exhausts, and all imported at huge expense in order to be driven in circles around the bandstand. Positioned on the pavement in front of the chamber orchestras that are there to provide a feeble accompaniment to songs being feebly sung, high-society Mexican horsemen – the so-called *charros* – are lined up boot-to-boot on horseback upon the pavement. The automobiles file past them as they give a languid salute, just like in *Cyrano*.[173] They are all dressed in traditional costume: tight blue-and-silver suede trousers, short jackets with braiding and the famous hats embroidered with gold. They are seated on their saddles, so-called *montura* saddles of buck-stitched tan leather, as though they were Pullman chairs, their feet in silver stirrups, a lasso at their knee. They smoke very black – *colorados* – cigars and are soon surrounded by blobs of the careless spittle that they cast down on the ground like alms.

Beneath the blaze of this February noon, beneath this sky that is never striped with rain, the monumental military and ecclesiastical grandeur of Spain towers over the grid of neatly aligned streets. It is clearly visible in the churches, governors' palaces and barracks, and in the fortified townhouses that only dynamite could demolish.

Mexico is America's oldest city. Its temples, palaces and tennis courts date from the twelfth century, when New York was still just a rock and was going to remain such for a long time, and when Buenos Aires was just savannah. From this belvedere I can see the towers of the cathedral built in the style that the

---

173 *Cyrano de Bergerac* is the title of a play (1897) by Edmond Rostand. The eponymous Cyrano was a real person, a Gascon nobleman soldier. In the play, he is a magnificent duelist, whose beloved accessory is a feather, or panache, and indeed the play is responsible for bringing this latter word into the English language, where it means 'aplomb'. Cyrano is afflicted with a very large nose which he fears will prove a stumbling block to the requital of his love for the beautiful Roxane.

Jesuits tortured just like they tortured those kings who refused to hand over their treasures. Their cathedral is built above the Great Temple and sacred Pyramid of the Aztecs, the idols from which were used to fill in the canals. This crude and absurd confection, built from roughly hewn rocks, had ousted an erudite and secret architecture from the same bloodline as Egyptian art. In front of the cathedral, the Square of the God of War, the Plumed Serpent, became the Square of the Assumption of the Virgin. At some future point, the Virgin will be dethroned in turn by the statue of some half-caste academic in a bronze blazer. And so the world marches forward, assassination after assassination. But the one thing that no human being can obliterate is the landscape. Nobody could blast away the embrace of this rocky semi-circle whose radius measures one hundred kilometres. Its curves are brought closer by the purity of the air, which is rarefied by the altitude. Compared with the quality of light in this voided atmosphere, the air of Greece is just fog. The two volcanoes, Popocatepeti and Iztaccihuatl, the Smoking Mountain and the Sleeping Woman, are the colour of grapes of Corinth[174]. They rise to more than five thousand metres in altitude, their two snow-tipped, cone-shaped peaks appearing to hang in mid-air.

This plateau, this central mesa, this uneven plain and these indented crests outlined in greenish blue are all hiding their riches, just as women fleeing a riot conceal their diamonds in their body and their gold in their hair. It's not for nothing that on the map Mexico is shaped like a cornucopia, or horn of plenty. Fruits, wines and trees form the vegetal treasure of the Tropics, but up in the highlands, where the surface gives nothing away, it turns out that a miser's treasure chest lies beneath the ground. It contains silver, gold, rubies, copper and gushing torrents of oil that make the mineral oils of Asia look like little sprays. And in addition, sulphur, marble and many other sorts of hard stone that

---

174 Black Corinth grapes are small and seedless and, when dried, are often called 'currants'.

the craters have spewed out. All that geological activity, all those volcanic rages, and nothing to show for it but a few perfect opals or turquoises. And in the same way, here, like everywhere else, it takes massive demographic migrations to produce a single artist. This country has been ransacked, plagued and eviscerated by the races that have successively inhabited it. Yet none of them were able to deplete it or even to suspect the scale of its wealth.

Mexico is a land like no other. New Spain, which – not even one hundred years ago – stretched from the Antilles to San Francisco, has been the meeting place of East and West, the refuge of Negroes and Chinese, of Whites and of Redskins. In this land without seasons, in any given month, some trees are in flower while others are going through autumn. It's a place of tall cacti, resembling the pipes of an organ; of Ford cars, stripped of their engines and drawn by mules; of cowboys, open-mouthed from the cold, who enter bars without dismounting from Arab horses with rib-cages enlarged by the altitude. This is a country of charred railway stations, where official signs state that 'The discharging of firearms is forbidden'. It's a land of empty locomotives propelled by revolutionaries over the ravines below; a land of pawn shops and of plutonium mines with underground chapels where the candles are always lit; a land of palaces made of basalt, diorite and serpentine. Mexico is a place where precious metals and human life have no value and where wealth has only ever brought unhappiness. Wasn't the entire West speaking through Cortés when he sent the following message to King Montezuma, amazing the king by this expression of greed for the yellow metal: 'The Spaniards are stricken with a fatal disease that only gold can cure.'

It's 9 a.m. and, beneath a tightly tautened sky, I'm walking in streets so crowded that the very houses are being pushed back. At this altitude, the sky-high oxygen levels make one feel light as a balloon, as well as banishing fatigue and reducing the need for sleep.

'Morning time is one big party.'

The author of the above quotation from the French is my guide here in Mexico, the Mexican Minister of Foreign Affairs Señor Don Genaro Estrada. Like all contemporary Mexican leaders, Estrada is not yet forty. He's a huge man, powerful, good-natured, a skilful politician, a great bibliophile and, in spite of all the foregoing, a cultured man. The first time I met him, he stood up with difficulty behind his ministerial desk, made of one big map of the Americas, and said to me, point blank:

'I'd really love to have seen that exhibition of Cocteau's drawings.'[175]

'Minister, I would be delighted to lend you the catalogue.'

'There's no need; I already have it,' came the swift reply, to which he added:

'What's become of Reverdy?'[176]

And then, as an afterthought:

'I absolutely adore the luxury edition of *La Pharmacienne* by Giraudoux.'[177] (Now this book had only just been published as I myself was leaving Paris.)

Estrada then proceeds to tell me that he reads every night, that he has arranged for books to be sent to him from Europe, including luxury editions, and that he has taken out subscriptions to 150 French and foreign journals. He has only been once to Paris in his whole life. This is no Latinate snob who wants to show that he knows his Paris. He's just a cultured, sensitive man who relishes ideas and who has books sent to him from France

---

175 Jean Cocteau (1889-1963) was a gifted writer, artist, designer and filmmaker. His most famous written work is the novel *Les Enfants terribles* (1929) and his most famous film is probably *La Belle et la bête* (1946). He was a friend of Morand's.

176 Philippe Reverdy (1889-1960) was a French poet whose work was at a slight angle to the three main poetic movements of his time: Surrealism, Dadaism and Cubism.

177 See above p. 41, note 31. 'La Pharmacienne' is a story from Giraudoux's first book, a 1909 collection of short stories published by Bernard Grasset and entitled *Provinciales*.

much as others would send for the choicest fruits.

Instead of dragging me off to some exhibition or library or museum or other, Estrada has me sit into his big, silent car and escorted, to begin with, through ever narrower streets right into the open market. And that's how I got to see the real Mexico, Mexico live. We passed within centimetres of Indians whose mongoloid features or hooked noses connected them with ancient funeral masks carved in volcanic stone. I had never before seen the entire harvest of a certain locality collected together in such a small space; the produce from the hot zone had been carried up to the top of the plateau, where it sat next to the harvest of the temperate belt; the tropical fish lay beside the mangoes, the red bananas, the radishes, the giant corncobs or indeed, the early fruits, which were far more beautiful than the ones awarded first prize in our shows at home. Estrada showed me whole pineapples selling for two cents.

'One day,' he said, 'I was having lunch in Paris at Voisin's.[178] I wanted to order a particularly sophisticated and refined dessert.' 'What would you say,' the Head Waiter replied, 'to a slice of pineapple?'

Genaro Estrada, author of the delicious *Pero Galín*[179], then dragged me off on a hunt for antiques, the kind of safari from which he is wont to return, like the hero of his book, laden down with the 'finds' that he so winningly terms *preciosidades*.

We brave the 'Thieves' Emporium', the *Velador*, a sort of flea market, housed in the former tennis court of the Aztecs. In the past, bulls and heretics were put to death here. Estrada, by what kind of guesswork did you glean exactly what would appeal to

---

178 Voisin's is the name of a restaurant that flourished in Paris at 261 on the corner of the Rue du Faubourg St Honoré and the Rue Cambon. It closed in 1930, but gave its prestigious name to another restaurant founded in 1913 in New York.

179 The novel *Pero Galín* was published in 1926. It satirizes the colonialist novel and is a good-natured critique of 'fake colonial' taste in general, an infatuation that led the eponymous hero to change his name from Pedro Galinda.

my taste? How often have I dodged a day in the office, heading off instead to the 'Rastro' in Madrid or the 'Caledonian Market' in London! And as for the market in Rome, is it my fault that I haunted it? It is located, after all, right in front of the Farnese Palace... What, then, could be more entrancing than the *Velador* of Mexico City, that Colonial Paradise (or indeed its younger brother, the market of the Lesser Lagoon)? Invisible gramophones sound grainily from behind racks of fur coats and from a stall selling old rusted nails emerges the pure voice of Mary Garden.[180] We pass then into the saddler quarter, Leatherware Street. The layout of the market has remained faithful to its Spanish origins and beneath the Spanish style I can make out the Arab *souk*. There are magnificent leather saddles for sale, embossed using heat or metal tools; also stirrups and bridles decorated with silver braiding. And rails of shoes, which Estrada likens, with the smile of a connoisseur, to bunches of bananas. Or sandals of white leather, like those worn by ancient philosophers. To the right, behind the used tyres, are the booksellers. They all greet my companion in low voices, showing him old Castilian theology books and even some incunabula[181], as well as books by the French Romantics. In the most beautiful corner of the market stands the hat stall. What a monumental folly it is for film directors to insist on filming inside the studios, even though these just repeat the ghastliness of stage sets. What a marvellous film set this marketplace would make! What a stellar line-out is formed by these huge Mexican straw hats, complete with freckles! Turned-up hats, flat-brimmed hats, cowboy hats – *vachero* or Córdoba style, in white felt or black fur, decorated with silver and gold, adorned with pompoms or bells... And then of course there are those extraordinary conical hatboxes

---

180 Mary Garden (1874-1967) was a Scottish opera singer who was chief soprano in the Opéra Comique in Paris during the first decade of the twentieth century. She moved to New York in 1907, spending the next twenty years of her career in America.
181 These are very early printed books (printed before 1501).

that require a whole train compartment for themselves. Seeing them for real, I'm forced to abandon all hope of being able to bring one back to France.

Estrada is already pulling me across the street where, in the past, the Holy Office used to process, bound for the stake. I only have time to glance briefly at the street of potters, at the beautiful modern Mexican pottery from Guadalajara, Puebla, Talavera, Zacatecas... Already I'm being dragged far away into a small church which opens out on to the street. Without uttering a word, Estrada pinches my arm. There before me, on a side altar, I see the strangest trio in black and white.

He explains that this is the Poisoned Christ, the *envenenado*, and beside him stand an angel and the Virgin of Solitude.

I had certainly seen many Black Christs in Spain, but never such a dreadful spectacle as now met my eyes. Imagine a life-size Christ, stumbling, collapsing, covered in black polish, with a Negro's face hidden behind the blond curls of real hair styled into the so-called *anglaises* or ringlets worn by our grandmothers. Beside him, in a hieratic pose and looking deathly white, the very essence of Solitude, the Virgin, stands erect and dry-eyed, twisting in her hands a delicate lace handkerchief as she awaits his agony with poison in her eyes.

'Are you familiar with the legend?' my companion inquires. 'A young girl, who had ingested poison by accident, threw herself down at the feet of this statue of Christ – who was white back then. As she prayed, full of trust and love, the miracle took place: bit by bit the statue absorbed the poison and in the end, after she had been saved, the white Christ had turned black...'

We now find ourselves facing the Grand Opera House of Mexico. It's still under construction and, as the elevation rises, its proud and top-heavy mass sinks down into the yielding ground. As a result, the gods will soon be at street level, just like in English theatres. We get jostled by authentically American traffic as we pass in front of former rococo palaces. They are painted in shades of old pink or potpourri and their protruding coats of arms are either covered in tightly curled carving or rejuvenated by the vivid blues and yellows of pieces of porcelain tiles. Inside, at the back of the courtyards, I can make out patios with granite colonnades and whitewashed walls, a central fountain and either an oleander or a palm tree climbing right up to the balconies. But now we have reached the famously beautiful corner house named *Casa de los Azulejos* (or the House of Tiles), the most comely colonial home in all the Americas. People in the United States would pay dearly to call it theirs. It was built in 1596 in the so-called *Mudéjar* style, which is Spanish in inspiration but steeped in the Arab aesthetic. The entire facade on two different streets is covered with *azulejos*, tiles of Puebla pottery, blue on a white background. This building now belongs to the Yturbe family.

In the narrow street that we turn into next, sweethearts are exchanging promises, Spanish-style, at the barred windows resembling cash counters in banks. The traditional serenades became extremely costly after the police started to raise a tax on every song. But the lovers still have at their disposal the free language of flowers, fans and handkerchiefs. Above all, they have the tax-free language of finger gestures, facial expressions and shrugs, the enchanted idiom that allows the beloved and her beau or *majo* to express their love simultaneously. And so the whole ancient culture of picaresque Spain, long extinct in Europe, lives on here.

My eye is caught by the heavy double entrance doors, with their three concentric arches: the lowest one, like a cat-flap, is for pedestrians; the medium one is for those on horseback; and the full opening is for carriages. I'm quite taken too with the peasants who are all wrapped up in *zarapes*. These are shawls made of woven wool that has been tinted with primitive vegetal dyes and striped with those rigid bands also seen on African cloth. As for the half-caste *caballeros*, they carry cigars in their mouths and blades, the weapon of choice, in their pockets. The language spoken by all these Mexicans is the beautiful Spanish of Cervantes; not, therefore, the typically bastardized tongue of South America, but the best American Castilian, embellished, however, with graceful Indian similes.

On the site of the temple of Quetzalcoatl, the God of War, lies the flower market. The flowers are arranged like a wreath around a pool. This wreath is even bigger than Mexican funereal wreaths, which themselves are taller than the coffins, making one wish one were dead in order to smell so good one last time. The cobblestones are strewn with roses, camellias, gardenias, and tuberoses[182], the full bounteous harvest of the Tropics. Other blooms, this time living ones, are also on sale here, namely equatorial birds (canaries and parrots in bamboo cages, blue and orange macaws), not to mention monkeys. The latter, perched on the shoulders of the vendors of lottery tickets, point to the relevant numbers…

The car stops in front of the Ministry of Public Education and I follow Estrada into the courtyard. It's a space as big as the central courtyard of the Sorbonne with a triple gallery running right around it. The walls are covered in frescoes from floor to ceiling. When I move closer, expecting to see some mournful academic allegory, I find myself facing instead a whole series of admirable compositions executed with extraordinary skill in a style at once simple and novel.

'It's the work of Diego Rivera,'[183] Estrada tells me. Rivera, currently America's foremost painter, worked for ten years in Paris and is now filling Mexico with his paintings. I was unable to meet with this powerful man, who prides himself on being a mere artisan, because he had just fallen from scaffolding. At

---

182 Tuberoses are tropical plants with large white funnel-shaped flowers.
183 Diego Rivera (1886-1957) was a Mexican painter whose world-renowned frescoes launched the Mexican muralist movement. He is also remembered for his radical political views on social equality and for his tempestuous relationship with the painter Frida Kahlo.

that point he was still between life and death, but fortunately he did make a full recovery. The huge, very moving compositions covering these walls represent popular scenes like Indian ceremonies and pagan rituals, but with such joie de vivre, such pictorial exhilaration and such affection for his country, for beautiful girls and Indian farm-hands. Black workers and redskin bodies dressed in startling white have yielded here naive art the likes of which one would probably be unable to find anywhere in Europe. Certainly, Paul Gauguin, Maurice Denis and more especially Georges Seurat[184] all took the same approach, and their example was not lost on Rivera. Yet, despite this, he managed to hang on to his own personality. Notwithstanding his literary and political influences, which include pacifism, the Hammer and the Sickle and the painterly style of the Barbussians[185], none of which add anything to his originality, the work of Diego Rivera offers not just a beautiful affirmation of art, but also an irrepressible optimism.

I cannot but congratulate the Education Minister, who is indeed very proud of the Ministry.

- How is it, I ask him, that in Mexico the decoration of an official building is entrusted to a talented artist who is so young and so audacious?

- It's because Mexico doesn't yet possess an Academy, comes

---

184 Paul Gauguin (1884-1903) was a French Post-Impressionist painter who is remembered mostly for his distinctive use of colour and for his paintings of Tahitian subjects. Maurice Denis (1870-1943) also belonged to the transition between Impressionism and modern art, and was tempted by Symbolist art and also by Neoclassicism for a time. Also identified as a Post-Impressionist painter, Georges Seurat (1859-1891) is mainly known for his use of a technique known as *pointillisme*, based on the rendering of light and colour through the use of very small dots of paint.

185 Morand is referring here to Rivera's politics: the Barbussians were those who admired the writings of Henri Barbusse (1873-1935), a pacifist and avowedly Communist writer: hence the allusion to the Hammer and Sickle, the symbols of socialism on the coat of arms of the Soviet Union.

the reply.

According to Mexican legend, a total of four suns prior to the present one have shone upon this earth. Each one marks a complete phase of the world's history, a cycle that ended in universal destruction. The first sun was supposed, according to Joyce[186], to have been inhabited by giants and devoured by jaguars; the second was populated by monkeys and annihilated by a hurricane; the third was destroyed by fire; the fourth by water, while the fifth, our own sun, will be destroyed by seismic shocks.

The names given to things by the ancient Aztec tribes were full of magic: 'the people who speak clearly'; the 'sowers of flowers'; the 'crossers of bridges'; the 'people of the curved mountain'; the 'people who turn their faces towards the earth'.

It was in the British Museum, around 1908, that I first discovered Mexican art, that is, the art pre-dating the Spanish Conquest: masks made of hard stone with eyes made of mother-of-pearl, obsidian or iron pyrite and cheeks made of incrusted turquoise. What I found appealing was not just their Mycenaean[187] grandeur, but also the beauty and exquisiteness of the material in which they were worked. I envied those English travellers who had managed to discover and acquire them around 1850. Especially fascinating for me was the famous Mexican death head in the British Museum, life size, carved from a single block of rock crystal. Since then, I've seen others in Paris and in Mexico City, but this one is truly unique. Indeed, I never pass through London without returning for another look. In 1918, I saw the pre-Cortés collection in the Archeological

---

186 Thomas Athol Joyce (1878-1942) was an English archeologist who worked for the British Museum. His book, *Mexican Archaeology*, appeared in 1914, just one year before an article for the *Encyclopaedia Britannica* stating the supposed 'mental inferiority' of the 'Negro' earned him much criticism.

187 The Mycenaean civilization of Ancient Greece corresponded to the last phase (about 500 years) of the Bronze Age.

Museum of Madrid, though it's only very recently that I got to see the American collection in the Musée du Trocadéro.[188] It was midday: in other words, I couldn't see a thing, although I did glimpse some real treasures in the museum's Mexican collections, the ones donated by the Duke of Lobat, by Mr Lirillar and by Messrs Charny and Génin. A few years ago Mr Génin[189], the head of Mexico's French colony and owner of a priceless collection, had stated his intention of returning to his practice of donating art to the French state. At first his offer met with no response at all, but he was eventually informed that his donations would only be accepted on condition that he himself pay for the display cabinets! When France is rich again, what a beautiful museum of Mexican art it will be able to afford, thanks to the contributions of experts such as Mr Rivet and the Society of Americanists.

Of course, with the single exception of the French volume, *Manual of American Archaeology*, authored by Beuchat and published in 1912, virtually the entire bibliography on the subject is in German. I used to dream at one time of going off to excavate the Yucatán, to dig up buried cities and discover lost civilizations in the jungle. Alas, my trip through Mexico has been all too short. There hasn't been time enough to travel down to the South and my sense of loss is made more acute by all that I now know. To be more precise, my dream of buried temples was no mirage; nor was my dream of cities just as mysterious as their Cambodian sister-cities still were fifty years ago. For every day brings new treasures to light.

It goes without saying that the museum in Mexico does

---

188 This museum, located in the Palais de Chaillot on the Avenue du Trocadéro in Paris, changed its name to the Musée de l'Homme.

189 Auguste Alexis Génin was born in 1862 and died in 1931 in Mexico, the son of a French father and Belgian mother. He was a businessman, an archeological explorer, a naturalist and a writer. He served as Honorary Belgian Consul in Mexico between 1905 and 1920 and he represented the Mexican tobacco industry at the Exposition Universelle in Paris in 1889.

not disappoint. In itself it is well worth a long detour. Without pausing even once for breath, I whizzed through its remarkable ethnographic and historical collections, its departments of fine arts and colonial artefacts and the charming portrait gallery dedicated to the viceroys of New Spain. The first few figures (from the sixteenth century) were dark and skinny like all hunters, while the later ones were pink and chubby like the hunters' prey. I eventually reached the ground floor where the most famous sculptures are to be found. Prior to arriving in Mexico, I had learnt off some dates, thinking that it would be no more difficult to situate in time the different civilizations of Mexico (Aztec, Toltec and Maya) than the various Greek dynasties. But once I arrived here, I learned to be sceptical. Whereas, for the period of Cortés, there's an abundance of documentation and transactions, for the preceding periods we're floundering in uncharted waters. The meaning of the great stone calendars can be made out thanks to their references to eclipses, which the Aztecs calculated with extraordinary precision. But when it comes to their writing, these strange ideograms are utterly opaque. The reproduction of the Damietta Stone[190] is a case in point. Mexico is still waiting for its own Champollion[191] to decipher the bilingual inscription that might explain the object. As I was standing beside two priests in ceremonial dress in front of the casts and bas-reliefs of the Temple of the Cross in Palenque, I overheard someone say that it would be impossible to tell whether they were sculpted before

---

190 What Morand refers to here as the Damietta Stone appears to be the Rosetta Stone. The two towns in Egypt are just eighty-three miles apart. Certainly, it was the Rosetta Stone that was discovered by Pierre Bouchard in 1799 during the Napoleonic campaign in Egypt and that was decoded by Champollion.

191 Champollion (1790-1832) was a French philologist and Orientalist who spoke Coptic and Arabic fluently and managed to decode the hieroglyphics of the trilingual Rosetta Stone (which also featured Greek and Demotic scripts), beginning around 1805. He showed, amongst other things, that the signs carved on the stone were both phonetic and ideographic.

or after our own era.

Regardless of all that, let's just allow ourselves to relish the pleasure (or the terror) of beholding these strange stone remains one by one. They are all so original and yet so closely related to the art of the Pacific and of China, and – via the Orient – to our own Romanesque art. These men were prodigious sculptors! In the pre-Aztec and Aztec eras their art was harshly realist, but it had been much more graceful and ornamental in Mayan times. Around the eighth century the Maya settled in the Yucatán, in the Mexican South, but also in present-day Guatemala and British Honduras. They seem to have mastered in one stroke that simplification of line and space so sought-after in modern art. They were surrounded by an abundance of the most beautiful, the rarest and most durable raw materials that the world can offer. And yet, right up to the arrival of the Spaniards, they knew nothing at all of metals (except bronze to a certain extent). This is why they had to sculpt the material so delicately, to polish it manually with such patience, to rub rather than pound or carve the granite mother-block. This is what gives their work its softness and the finish of natural wear and tear, so utterly different to the clinical cuts of the chisel or the arbitrary assault with an iron tool. Hence this unheard-of phenomenon: the emergence of a pre-historic Stone-Age art in our own historic times.

Concerning statuary in the strict sense of the term, pieces like the 'Dead Man's Head', sculpted in basalt in the pre-Aztec era, or the 'Man's Head in an Eagle's Beak', both of which are on display in Mexico City, show a powerfulness that was admired but never equaled by Rodin (or so I've been told). In contrast, the seated figure of Xochipilli, the God of Flowers, a sort of masked Bacchus carved in red basalt and dressed in animal skins, has the grace of a Maillol or a Carpeaux.[192] The Aztecs and their predecessors were also incomparably skilled as carvers of animals. Mexico comes second only to India in this endeavor and in both cases the decorative motifs all seem to have been inspired by the snake. Whether it's wound up in a spiral, whether it lies unwound all along the length of the sculpted friezes and whether it's covered in scales or in feathers, the Mexican snake resembles no other serpent. Similarly, eagles, jaguars, wolves, turtles and shells are all depicted with the same stunning magnificence and simplicity. What is most especially impressive in this aesthetic is the geometric rigour and the architectural sensibility. In other words, form and shape are always subordinated to the particular attributes of the material. The sculpture deliberately follows the lines suggested by nature itself, just as the imagination of the poet embraces metrical constraint. Nothing seems to confound the Aztec artist, neither the sharpness of the angles nor even the limitations of the available surface area. He makes nothing of such challenges and may even seek them out.

How might we describe the Aztec Calendar, the so-called 'Sun Stone'? The Aztecs brought it with them from somewhere in the North, but no one knows whence exactly. It was buried, of course, by the Spaniards, when they were building their cathedral. Unearthed in the seventeenth century by the (second) Archbishop de Montúfar[193], it was immediately reinterred, so great was the fear that the Indians might revert to their idolatry.

---

192 Aristide Maillol (1861-1944) was a painter and printmaker as well as a sculptor, whose statues are mostly based on the female body ('Air' or 'The River') and were precursors to the work of Henry Moore. Jean-Baptiste Carpeaux (1827-75) was also a sculptor in Second-Empire Paris. Admiring the baroque tradition, he broke with classicism. His works were commissioned for the Palais Garnier opera house in Paris and for the 'Pavillon de Flore' at the Louvre Palace.

193 Alonso de Montúfar was a Spanish Dominican friar who was born in Granada in 1489 and served as second Archbishop of Mexico between 1555 and 1572. Devotion to Our Lady of Guadelupe was initiated and promoted during his time as archbishop.

The first Bishop of Mexico ordered for his part the destruction of twenty thousand statues in one year. And when the Dominican father, Benito Fernández[194], found amongst these an emerald four fingers long and two fingers wide, representing a bird entwined by a snake, he smashed it into smithereens. The Calendar was unearthed again in 1790. It's a huge millstone with a frieze sculpted in porphyritic basalt around its circumference. Unfortunately I wasn't able to see it properly because a cast was being taken during my visit and the frieze had been entirely covered with a thick layer of plaster. Where did these ancestral Aztecs learn about astronomy? Where did they obtain the knowledge that inspired this design, based as it is on the four key symbols: wind, water, earth and fire? That knowledge also dictated the seven circles into which the monolith is divided, each one subdivided in turn into months and days, following the very similar data of Assyrian and Babylonian science, albeit a more perfected version of these.

And what about the Sacrifice Stone, a monument dedicated to the Sun by King Tizoc?[195] This is a sort of Trajan Column[196], a cylinder of basalt. Its carvings depict victims being dragged by the hair to the column itself, then laid down upon this very stone where their hearts were torn out with a knife made of black obsidian.

The 'Statue of the Setting Sun', Tonatiuh, is a sacred mask surrounded by sunrays, while the 'Statue of Chalchiuhtlicue', the

---

194 *Letters and Memorials of the Father Presidente Benito Fernández de Santa Ana 1736-54*, ed. and trans. Benedict Leutenegger, San Antonio, Texas: Our Lady of the Lake University, 1981.

195 Tizoc (Tizocic) ruled Tenochtitlan from 1481 to 1486. He was a grandson of Moctezuma I and Itzcoatl.

196 Trajan was of combined Italian and Iberian origin and was Emperor of Rome between 98 and 117 AD. He presided over the greatest military expansion ever of the Roman Empire and was also known as a great builder. The Trajan Column is a free-standing carved victory column completed in 113 AD; it celebrates the Roman victory in the Dacian wars (waged over present-day Romania and Moldova).

Moon Goddess, is a twenty-two thousand kilo monolith with a flat facade. Both possess that malevolent power sometimes adumbrated in Negro art. However, it is the way in which Death is represented that most clearly and weirdly distinguishes Aztec art. No longer do we find the youthful, spindly image of Death as depicted on Etruscan vases. Instead it's the Colossus to which the Indians of Mexico still refer as 'the Lion tamer'. And so the Monument to Death stands upon a pedestal formed by a massive block of volcanic rock with a topping of skulls and crossed bones scattered all over it. And as for the monstrous statues of the Goddess of Death, Mictecacihuatl[197], of which there are seven or eight in the museum, these are huddled shapes with their claws outstretched, ready to take flight. Their staring eyes, bulging out of their sockets, are unconsciously imitated by the contemporary indigenous art of origami, beloved of those feasts and carnivals where everybody, in order to partake in the singing and entertainment, has to wear a Death mask. I should mention in this connection Roberto Montenegro's excellent study on the history of the American mask, a prehistoric tradition upheld throughout the entire colonial period.[198] Just like in Hindu cosmography, for the Aztecs the Goddess of Death is also the Goddess of the Earth and of Humankind. And indeed, when we look at the museum's most extraordinary statue, we could be looking at Kali.[199] It's a primitive block of stone four metres high, with a head comprising two snake heads facing one another and a body festooned with magic pendants: skulls, severed hands and extracted hearts.

---

197 Mictecacihuatl was the Aztec goddess of death. She inhabited Mictlan, the Aztec underworld, with her husband, another deity called Mictlantecuhtli.

198 Roberto Montenegro Nervo (1885-1968) was an artist and a friend of Diego Rivera. Like the latter, he was one of the principal painters of the Mexican muralist movement.

199 Kali is worshipped by Hindus as the divine protectress, mother of the universe and destroyer of evil forces. She is often depicted standing or dancing upon the prostrate body of her consort, Shiva.

One and a half hours by car away from Mexico City, we are driving along the last mud-flats, vestiges of the ancient Lake Texcoco. In the distance lies a collapsed aqueduct and a number of watchtowers stand on the hilltops. The countryside is old, worn-out and wrinkled. It's an expanse of desert with a relief that looks either unfinished, or else flattened out by erosion. Nothing grows here apart from the leafless trees, or the strange-shaped cacti that surround the houses like hairy fences. It's a land without water and its soil is more mineral than vegetal in composition. Eventually, the horizon contracts on all sides as the plain of Mexico City is enclosed by the violet-hued mountains that we're about to approach. Then suddenly the road disappears and straight ahead of us a tall grey pyramid looms up in the bleaching air of noon. It's not as tall as the Egyptian pyramid but it has a broader base. This is the Pyramid of the Sun, Teotihuacan.

The monument rises in five stages or levels and can be climbed either by a single or by a double stairs. The steps separate and join up again the whole way up to the top. They are steep and narrow (a fact that, from a distance, underlines the effects of perspective and makes the climb very difficult, requiring that one simultaneously twist one's feet and stoop). I climb without stopping to rest, even though I'm weighed down by all the Mexican loose change that will be paying for our taxi this evening. The *peso* is the legal tender here and it's as weighty as its name suggests. What a spectacle this sacred enclosure must have presented in the past, as celebrants wielding axes of chalcedony and priestesses with white down stuck onto their skin climbed so high above the plain, right up to the statue of the Sun, carved in porphyry and surrounded by burning joss-sticks. At that time, the monument was covered in red stucco and resembled a geometrical inferno. Everything here is on a titanic scale: the purity of the sky is infinite and the silent landscape is weightless, devoid of sin and want, marked only by the blots made by the two volcanoes topped by cones of pink snow.

To the left lies another pyramid, a smaller one, the Pyramid of the Moon. It's still not entirely cleared of the mask of earth and dust that once hid it from view and it offers a curious contrast with the dry, austere lines of its elder sister. The Mexican government has had the latter completely restored, some would say over-restored in fact. On the morning of my arrival I had seen both of them from the railway, bathed in the light of the rising sun. They hadn't, however, seemed to me as beautiful then as now, in the full blast of the blazing heat of the solar furnace. In this place there is no interval between prayer and heaven. Whereas the Gothic spire is a leap towards God and the Egyptian pyramid is a dark well that sinks towards Hell and darkness, the Aztec pyramid is quite different. It's a temple to be ascended, a stone plateau clad in an earthen coat. On the summit, the celebrant is on the same level as the gods and the stars, just like the Chinese emperor standing atop the Temple of the Sky. But the Peking edifice, which is smaller and packed close against the earth, is a reconstruction and cannot compare with the hieratic simplicity and purity of style of the Mexican monument. To which era does it belong? One prior to the Christian age, certainly. As is the case for all the greatest geological puzzles that have remained to this day unsolved, estimates vary enormously. It could conceivably date back to ten centuries before Jesus Christ. Certainly, it significantly predates the Aztecs. These pyramids, devoid as they are of hieroglyphs, have yet to yield their secret. Will they ever reveal their story? Their discovery is still very recent: after all, they were only exhumed about ten to fifteen years ago. I've been told that even the Spanish *conquistadores* knew nothing about them. Who could have imagined that they were lying there, hidden beneath the grass, like the Palatine Hill[200] in the Middle Ages?

---

200 Rising about forty metres above the Roman Forum, this mound is the most central of Rome's seven famous hills.

The Way of the Dead leads to the Pyramid of the Moon, which – like the Pyramid of the Sun – is topped by a statue, the one that we admired in Mexico City, the statue of Chalchiuhtlicue.[201] This monolith, which weighs twenty-two thousand kilos, represents the Moon Goddess as a flat, mild and terrifying face, just like the Moon itself. It's reminiscent of the statue of the three-headed god Bayon, in Angkor.[202]

Several English scholars have written weighty tomes purporting to prove the connection between Egyptian and Aztec art. Yet they have failed to solve the riddle of these two sister pyramids. The recent paper from Messrs de Créqui-Montfort and Rivet is more impressive still.[203] In the Uru language of the Bolivian Indians, brothers to the Aztecs, the moon is called 'Isis'. And as we know, in Egypt, Isis is the Goddess of the Moon.

Beyond the two sister pyramids lies the Temple of Quetzalcoatl, the quintessential Mexican divinity, God of Air and of War. This is a vast quadrilateral covering sixteen hectares. It's positioned in a ritual axis joining the four cardinal points. Thanks to its stairways, its sheer slopes and its central altar – as stocky as an ammunitions store – it resembles the exposed slopes leading to a fortress. One almost expects to see the protruding canons of the Seville foundry bearing the coat of arms of Ferdinand VII.[204] The reason for its high-definition resemblance to an artist's impression is its recent restoration or reconstitution by contemporary architects. Yet,

---

201 Chalchiuhtlicue is the fertility-bearing Aztec Goddess of Water, whose name translates as 'Woman in a Jade Skirt'.

202 Bayon is a twelfth-century, richly decorated Khmer temple in present-day Cambodia, at Angkor. The huge faces carved into the rock towers of the temple were once held to represent Hindu gods but are now believed to celebrate the revered Buddhist King Jayavarman VII.

203 G. de Créqui-Montfort and P. Rivet were co-authors of several studies of Bolivian linguistics published by the French Société de Linguistique de Paris and by the *International Journal of American Linguistics* between 1916 and 1920.

204 Ferdinand VII, born in 1784 was King of Spain briefly in 1808, when he was overthrown by Napoleon I. He ruled again from 1813 to his death in 1833.

although the concrete is too recent and the stone too hard, all these cavils fade to nothing in the great melody sung by the overall proportions. If you squint, the temple recovers its timelessness and its place in the natural setting of mountains and sky. The only regret one could have is that the restoration work wasn't more comprehensive and that the temple walls weren't covered with red rendering (after all, on the northern side, vestiges of the original multi-coloured stucco-work are still visible). Behind the main altar the most amazing surprise lies in wait for the visitor: namely another, more archaic slab like the Korai[205] altar lying beneath the Acropolis of Pericles. From this point, a stairway leads down to two terraces, decorated with stylized tigers and owls, whose bulging sculpted eyes are almost Romanesque, though they also have a Sasanian look about them.[206] What are the traditions or beliefs that lay behind this art, this civilization that disappeared, leaving behind secrets whose mysteries had already become impenetrable no doubt for the Indians of the time of Cortés?

The steep slopes and fortress-like profiles of these Teotihuacan temples are clearly visible in the models and reproductions in the museum of Mexico City. These features are shared with the monuments of Chichén-Itzá[207] or Palenque[208], which themselves resemble the temples of Mitla[209] because of

---

205 Maiden in Greek is *kore*, plural *korai*. This altar features draped maidens. The Acropolis is in Athens and dates from the city's Golden Age (460-430 BC).

206 The Sasanian Empire was a third- to seventh-century AD Persian dynasty extending (prior to Arab conquest) over a vast territory that included present-day Armenia. It corresponds to a political and aesthetic Golden Age, its art typically representing figures with wide-open eyes, a very distinctive facial symmetry and geometrical hairstyles.

207 Chichén-Itzá is a major site of Mayan ruins (temples, pyramids, etc), located on the Yucatán Peninsula.

208 Palenque was a Maya city-state in Chiapas, Southern Mexico, with ruins dating from the second century BC to the eighth century AD.

209 Mitla is a highly significant archaeological site in the Mexican state of Oaxaca.

their Greek fret decoration and totemic ornamentation. They are also reminiscent of the architecture of India and even of the Chaldea.[210] In many detailed respects they seem related to the art of the Pacific as well. It is commonly believed that the Aztecs came from the North, from Alaska, that is to say from Asia. And we must not forget that there are scarcely fifty miles between America and Asia, between Alaska and Kamchatka[211], or that the warm Kuroshio current travels from Japan to America at a speed of between twenty and one hundred miles an hour. Humboldt[212] himself pointed out the affinities linking the inhabitants of opposite sides of the Pacific and it is indeed self-evident that a common aesthetic unites the entire Pacific Basin. Some American experts have even suggested that there may have existed, in the South Seas, a continent, a vanished land mass just like Atlantis. Even if we confine ourselves to historical time, how could we not be struck by the existence of so many traits shared by the Malaysians, the Negroes of Africa and the primitive Mexicans? Just think, for example, of the Aztec Calendar, which is still in use in Java. Or of the divine dimension attributed to birds of prey and the adoration of the snake. There are so many similarities between the different rituals, both funerary rites (painting the corpse red, for example) and other beliefs and practices like the religious, metaphysical and political supremacy of the female principle over the male, which prevails not just in early Japan and Mexico, but also, right down to the present day, in Sumatran[213] matriarchies. Not to mention the custom of planing the head into a sugarloaf shape. This practice

---

210 The Chaldeans were a Semitic people who inhabited an area of Mesopotamia between the ninth and sixth centuries BC.

211 Kamchatka is a volcanic region of far-eastern Russia.

212 Alexander von Humboldt (1769-1859) was a Prussian polymath, a geographer and climatologist but also an explorer and naturalist, who travelled widely in Latin America between 1799 and 1804.

213 Sumatra is a large Indonesian island located south of the Malaysian peninsula and to the west of Java.

so astonished the Spaniards that, when they saw the Aztecs for the first time, they were moved to call them 'heaped-up heads'.[214]

The terrible storm that ravaged the Pacific coast on February 20th 1927[215] was followed by floods that revealed a forgotten city, twenty miles long, beside Tixmucin in the State of Campeche. Several pyramids pre-dating the Mayan period, hitherto covered in stone, were discovered there, separated from one another by wide streets. The river that runs through the city is crossed by high stone bridges and its banks are strewn with carved stone utensils deposited there by the water. This city must significantly predate the great Maya-Toltec metropolis of Chichén-Itzá, which the Carnegie team is currently excavating. It seems increasingly likely, then, that thousands of years before the arrival of the Maya in the Yucatán, a splendid civilization was flourishing in the State of Campeche. No doubt many ruins remain to be explored there, including those currently covered up by nature and known only to jaguars.

In the early hours of the morning we left Mexico for Puebla, clearing the vast central plateau and reaching the mountains in a single thrust of the throttle. One hundred kilometres away from Puebla, the plain of Mexico is already receding – along with its airfield and its swamps fringed with saltpetre. The air is becoming cooler and the cacti have given way to pine trees. We've now reached the Río-Frío pass at more than three thousand metres altitude. The two staid volcanoes, which at first appeared in single file, now seem to stand side by side, allowing us to approach them up close. We can see their bizarre chimneys,

---

214 The expression used here by Morand is *cabezas apilonadas*, which suggests a 'piled up' or 'heaped up' head-shape. It is known that head-flattening (or head-binding) was practised by the Aztecs, Incas and Mayans. This practice of planing the front of the head pushed the skull bones and other matter backwards and upwards.

215 No trace of this storm and no trace of a place called Tixmucin can be found in any of the relevant historical or geographical documents consulted.

their lateral cones and adventitious craters. Beneath the tropical sun, the snow takes on an unfamiliar harshness of definition. In the evening, when we are leaving, it will have become vaporous again in the moonlight and the two bluish cones, floating in the high skies, will produce what people who cannot dream are wont to call a 'dream landscape'. As all the Mexican volcanoes are married, their white heads are always paired off. Thus Popocatepetl stands shoulder to shoulder with Iztaccihuatl, Perote's 'Treasure Chest' with Orizaba's Peak and Nevado de Colima with the Volcán de Colima.[216] On the other side of the pass, a different plain stretches out beneath the Sierra Madre and in the shade of another volcano, Matlalcueitl. On the tilled land of this plateau, the fortified *haciendas* have those crenellated towers with arrow slits so reminiscent of the *douars* and *bordjs* of French North Africa.[217] And everywhere there are churches and yet more churches! Acting under the impetus of a dark fanaticism and a neurotic mysticism, the Spaniards constructed churches in Mexico with no regard for the needs of the local religion or of the local population. However, the religious architectural style favoured by the *conquistadores* presents a curious contrast to this fierceness. It's an idiom that pushes to their furthest extreme both an extroverted gracefulness and a pleasing architectural flow. Wherever idols had been torn down, wherever an Aztec temple had stood, the air was regarded as having once been poisoned and so an altar had to be built there to proclaim the true God. Thus, there is no part of the landscape where the eye cannot make out the pink, ochre or pistachio-coloured shape of a church boasting white stucco motifs. Prior to arriving in Puebla, we drive through Cholula, an ancient holy city of the Aztecs, located in

---

216 Cofre de Perote is a massive chest-shaped volcano that is part of a long volcanic chain extending southward to Pico de Orizaba.

217 A *douar* (from the Arabic for 'tent') is a camp or settlement of tents, while *bordj* is the word for an Ottoman military citadel in Algeria. The Spanish word *hacienda* signifies a colonial estate.

Anahuac.[218] In the sixteenth century the Spanish earmarked this spot for a new conglomeration. However, since the expected population of one hundred thousand souls never turned up, the site resembles one of those beach resorts dreamed up by some unfortunate property speculator. All that remains of it today is a field of pointed-leaf agave plants stretching out as far as the eye can see. The right angles of the planned roads are still visible in the middle of the countryside and, in each planned district of the future city, a church was built in advance. And so it is that this inanimate plain, inhabited only by lizards, boasts between fifty and one hundred churches still awaiting congregations that will not be flocking there anytime soon. Nearby, the extant Aztec pyramid resembles an artificial acropolis crushed like a snake by a statue of the Virgin of Cures and Remedies. From this vantage point, the Spanish city of Puebla, rival to Cholula[219], is clearly visible: city of a thousand crinolines and a thousand churches, the Rome of Mexico.

When the archbishop passes nobody genuflects any more, as they used to have to do, or else risk being fined. Yet Puebla is still as picturesque as ever and its streets are still full of theatrical plotting. The city is paved by uneven cobblestones reminiscent of the poorer quarters of Madrid and decorated by the multi-coloured pottery that has made its reputation. Having crossed North Africa and Andalusia, the art of Persia has ended up here, having followed one of those vast, stumbling trajectories that fate imposes on entire peoples. This explains the presence of domes the colour of corn on the cob; of lanterns topped by green stripes in angular patterns like herringbone parquet; and of shining chapel spires corseted within yellow tiles striped with black, like wasps in the azure sky, buzzing beside fountains of blue… Such

---

218 Anahuac is the name (meaning 'close to water') that was given to the core of Mexico, a vague area corresponding to about three-quarters of the present day republic.

219 Cholula and Puebla de Zaragoza are both cities located close to one another in the central Mexican state of Puebla.

were the gambols and frolics of the ingeniously joyous art that flourished beneath the laughing sky of Mexico.

Rivalling its sister edifice in Mexico City, the Cathedral of Puebla towers in high colonial style above the plain, much as the Cathedral of Chartres presides over the Beauce.[220] Inside, the cathedral is a museum of wrought ironwork and precious wood, though its religious painting, like that of the country as a whole, is worthless. If the Indians knew nothing at all about vaults when the Spaniards arrived, afterwards they lost no opportunity to copy their colonial masters. As a result, the cathedral abounds in curves, arcades, arches and domes: they are everywhere. I don't spend much time looking at the marquetry work of the stalls or at the beautiful sacristy tables with their shell and spiral shapes. Yet these are being snapped up all over Mexico to decorate the atria of American millionaires. For me, what is sublime here are the golden gates that lead, Spanish-style, as in Seville and Barcelona, to each lateral chapel and also to the choir. This Mexican gold is a truly wondrous material. In quality and in colour, it looks like the purest of metal ingots, hammered into shape like Scythian armour. In reality, though, it's as tough and resistant as Carolingian jewellery. Nowhere else in the world did art encounter conditions as favourable as these: not just free, naturally gifted indigenous labour, but such a huge abundance of raw materials that these could scarcely be termed rare or precious. As for the faith of the *conquistadores* in their artistic project, suffice it to say that the effort or time that it required counted no more for them than they had counted for the Pharaohs. After all, the already fanatical religious faith of Castile and Aragon had already joined forces in Spain with the Muslim imperative to affirm the existence of God.

Since there was no chance of encountering an external obstacle that might impose some limits on the project, the *conquistadores*

---

220 The Beauce region of France is flat and boasts so many huge wheat-fields that it is known as the country's bread basket.

succumbed to the temptation of the baroque. Hence the Mexican *churrigueresque*[221], a style of charming extravagance that effortlessly seduces the modern taste of our age, an age all too rapidly sanitized, then sapped by the austerity of worship in medieval and immediately post-medieval times. In Europe only the Manueline[222] flourish of the Portuguese could rival with such debauchery of monumental style. The Franciscans distinguished themselves in this respect, with the Church of San Francisco presenting the most stunning and spectacular case in point. It has ceilings weighed down with stalactites that seem to have been sculpted with a curling tongs; and its swollen wrought-iron gates and other iron work are decorated with the sundry spirals and unwarranted swirls that resemble the signature of a lunatic. As for its pillars, they appear to be on the point of collapsing beneath the decorative overload. Not only is the entire confection gleaming in gold-leaf, but the High Altar is covered with a marquetry in onyx and rare marble that is echoed in other features. It adorns the floors of tropical wood, the confessionals twisting under the weight of baroque sins and the lecterns that look like the silver carriages that one might see in Lisbon, originally made for an embassy in Rome but which never got as far as the Holy See. All in all, this church left me with an impression of bemused bedazzlement.

We climb up onto a peak with a view over all of Puebla. At our feet lies a wasteland that is of no financial value whatsoever (although it's hard to imagine any land lying so close to the United States being financially worthless). It's from this sloping desert, marked by the gouged-out beds of waterfalls, that the

---

221 *Churrigueresque* architecture is highly ornamental, integrating a great deal of sculpture. It is most frequently found in the design of facades and of altars.

222 Manueline architecture is a late Portuguese Gothic style, full of sumptuous flourish and incorporating maritime influences.

first French assault was led in 1862[223], resulting in a defeat. And this is why May 5th, the anniversary of this Mexican victory, is Mexico's National Feast Day.

All the domes of this holy city are being baked relentlessly by the straight rays of the sun. On the other side of the plain looms another mountain, a higher one, from which the French launched another attack, this time subduing the city. In the museum at Puebla there are some very moving wood engravings, where the trousers of our soldiers are like pools of blood amongst the cacti: 'Oy, Mexicanos!' As I head back to the city for lunch, I reflect on our campaign and especially on what it had in common with so many other examples from French military history: namely a courage born of ignorance and of supreme confidence in technical resources that were in reality inadequate. Yet it must be said that the expedition was not devoid of political significance. It was clear from the start that the North American colonies, having risen up against England, would never again accept submission to a European monopoly. And yet one might have hoped that the former Spanish colonies would one day bow again to European rule. For France in 1860, the idea of a greater sphere of French monarchic influence would have had the merit of containing the younger and still weak southern States in the same way that Canada was holding the northern territories in check. The idea was in essence a return to Louis XIV's dream of taking New Orleans and the mouth of the Mississippi. But the success of the mission would have depended on support

---

223 The Franco-Mexican war (also called the Second French Intervention or the Maximilian adventure) lasted from 1861 to 1867 and ended with a definitive victory for the Mexican Republic. A (Second Empire) French initiative under Napoléon III, the attack on Mexico was initially presented as a pan-European response to bad Mexican debts and was for a short time supported by the Spanish and the British as a venture intended to secure free trade for Europe within Latin America. An Austrian archduke (Maximilian Ferdinand) was made emperor by the French in 1864 but he was assassinated and the Mexican republic was restored in 1867.

from local conservative elements, that is to say from the pope. Whereas in fact Maximilian embarked on this venture without a papal concordat and, as everybody knows, the Vatican never did back him up. Of course, now that all the Mexican churches are either bolted up or else inhabited by turkeys and mangy dogs, Rome can rue its stance at leisure. So also can the big Mexican landowners, who were summarily evicted, never to return. They too had had their day.

That morning, we had lunch in Puebla at Père Magloire's. This French restaurant goes right back to the aforementioned heroic days of French supremacy and indeed its cellar – oh bliss! – still boasts some extraordinary wines. The Burgundies, of course, have become insipid, like faded pastels, whereas the Bordeaux wines are bearing up. Although their corks are ready to crumble into powder, the alcohol still holds its punch in its glassy fortress. The liqueurs of Père Magloire remain my very best memory of Puebla, especially one stupendous tea liqueur, made from an old Creole recipe. Verily, my travels have not been in vain!

I love the desert. The trees are never more than fifty centimetres tall and are still trying to look like corals. After all, this sandy expanse was once the sea bed and is today of a piece, of course, with the immense, border-defying Central American desert. After thirty hours of driving it will become the Sonoran desert; after forty, the desert of Arizona and after fifty the desert of Colorado. In reality, however, it's the self-same landscape all the way. On the horizon looms a mountain chain whose only function is to frame the picture in a blue reminiscent of these mosaics made from humming-bird feathers, a technique known to the Aztecs long before it was used by the Chinese.

I do, of course, long for water, even the bitter, salty water of Texcoco. My kingdom for a fish! The gusts of sandstorms have started to move through the Pullman compartment of the train[224], despite the double glazing of the closed windows and the chassis of sheet metal.

Zacatecas. San Luis Potosí. We're now approaching the border with the USA. This is classic smuggler country, beloved of the Apaches and Comanches. The name 'Apache' comes from a word meaning 'enemy' in the Indian dialect *Pima*, although the name of the Apache tribe translates literally as 'men of wood'. Having passed through Chihuahua, where the government troops are hunting down rebel Indians at present, we are now making our way through a landscape of sand dunes. A little further on, the meagre waters of the Rio Grande will form a (fictional) border between Mexico and the United States. Few travellers come this way apart from those heading for California. The shortest seven-day route from Mexico to New York passes through Laredo and San Antonio and it lies much further east. Here, at last, is the final Mexican town before the US: Ciudad Juárez. Two days have passed since we left Mexico City and we've been driving without a break ever since.

Like all the border towns encircling the United States, Ciudad Juárez has been experiencing extraordinary prosperity since Prohibition.[225] Its log houses are in reality white bars. They all sport coloured flags and are all sheltering apprentice millionaires. Each weekend Yankees throng here to siphon up beer, whisky and gin. Who wouldn't pay two or three hundred thousand *pesos* for such delights? The queue of cars is so long that one wonders how the bridge between the two nations is still holding up. Cards are being played with bottles of brown sauce on the table, just like in the films. I never saw so many ugly faces in one place as in the railway station of Ciudad Juárez.

---

224 Morand seems to be somewhat confused here as to whether he is travelling by car or by train.

225 Prohibition was in force in the USA from 1920 to 1933. What was outlawed was the production, importation, transportation, possession, sale and consumption of alcohol.

The places where merchandise, race and adventure mix best are the places where bottles are emptied and where the dregs of humanity are to be found. This is where undesirables and deportees congregate, waiting for their moment of opportunity. Just like the United States, all the countries of America, both North and South, are placing the most severe restrictions upon entry onto their territory. In Cuba I saw men whose papers were actually in order being sent back to Spain because they had an eye disease. No single women and no married women unaccompanied by their husbands can gain entry into Mexico. Everywhere, vaccination is obligatory. As for the United States, everybody knows what an impregnable barrier they erected around themselves from 1923 to 1925. There are, first of all, entry quotas for each race and these vary from year to year. Then there's selection on the basis of public health. A man missing some teeth, for example, will not be let in. Minimal disposable funds are also obligatory (about ten thousand francs). And on top of all that, they conduct a very strict assessment of morals, level of education, professional skills and even political leaning. 'Are you committed to not harming American society? If not, away with you!'

America is showing how a given race can improve its health and defend its purity and we must not forget its good example. Entering the United States is a privilege. We French should also patrol our own borders instead of perpetuating the fiction of the passport, a mere formality that can be side-stepped by the most basic of border subterfuges. Who hasn't heard of the Hendaye tram, the main roads of Charleroi or the trick with the Menton bus?[226] Regardless of the expense, we need to form a strong alien detection unit within our police force. This

---

226 A Belgian railway line (the 130A), which was completed in 1852 connects Charleroi in Belgium with France, while the tram from Hendaye in France to San Sebastián crosses the border with Spain. Likewise, a local bus-route from Menton crosses the border between France and Monaco.

needs to be an elite commando, entirely separate from those unfortunate *gendarmes* who wouldn't be able to tell apart an Eskimo and an Arab. Our models ought to be not only the USA, but also England, Italy and Germany. As for Russia, it's another case in point. France, which appeals to sentimental and outdated defences such as the 'right to asylum', the unrestricted right of any foreigner at all to admission, residence and political protection or indeed the short-term needs of the agricultural, hospitality or tourism industries, is the very last country in the world to practise such 'self-defence'. As a result our country has become a rag and bone shop. In a hundred years' time, what will our race have become? French life in its entirety revolves around a balance between South and North. Over the past century, this balance has been broken. So although the new blood we need is Celtic, Saxon and Germanic, instead we are opening the door to the Levant, to Semitic and Berber people and to the Latins from southern Europe, all those races of future traffickers and politicos.

The confidential instructions given to American consuls recommend that immigrants accepted from France be confined to men born north of the Loire. This racial balancing is no utopia: all the countries of Latin America, countries constituted by immigration, practise the same sort of quota system as that applied in the United States. Recently a Chilean minister told me in conversation that in 1925, Chile was limiting immigration to Scandinavians because 'theirs is the kind of heavy, serious, diligent blood that is needed here in the South.' 'We should be able to open and close our border like a tap,' he said.

On the other side of Ciudad Juárez and the Rio Grande lie the United States and El Paso. In a heartbeat we're surrounded by water, electricity, skyscrapers, enamel paint, tar macadam, ice-cream sodas, tortoiseshell glasses and newspaper supplements. The contrast is all the more startling because the city is surrounded on all sides by the self-same desert environment. Yet water gushes into all its bathtubs and on each hotel table lies a complimentary copy of the Bible, provided by the Gideons, the Christian society for commercial travellers. When we were travelling along the rough Mexican trails we yearned for the tender comforts of American highways. Yet no sooner have we been drawn beneath the great Yankee steamroller than we find ourselves starting to dream of the charming twists and turns of Mexico. But then, isn't that the fundamental rhythm of human life itself, which – like everything else in nature – is based on alternation? Happy then the traveller who, rather than choosing one or other extreme, lets himself be rocked by the constant swinging forwards and backwards of the pendulum.

This morning's newspaper[227] has the following report on the first page:

> 'A search has just been carried out in the home of Mr L., where it was found that certain well brought up young men, instead of going to high school, were spending their days lying about on sofas and snorting cocaine. Here we have an example of the damage done to teenagers by civilization, a by-word for modernism ... etc.'

However, moving on to page seven of the same publication, I read the following:

> 'In the context of an expedition up the Orinoco river, the explorer, Dr H.S. Dicking, has just discovered a hitherto unknown tribe of Indians, the Cuiapo-Pihibi. These Indians are perhaps the last completely savage race of human beings. They spend their days stretched

---

227 The newspaper is the *New York Times* (February 1929) and the report is titled 'A Visit to a Newly-Discovered Tribe: Mrs Dickey'. The author is Dr Herbert Spencer Dickey (not Dicking, as Morand writes), although Dr Dickey's wife is also prominently named and indeed pictured in the report, which was also carried by the English journal *The Sphere* on June 29th, 1929.

out sleeping or smoking cocaine in pipes made from hollowed-out deer bones.'

We are now making our way down the coast on the railroad.

Behold the American train! Its carriages are so high that the steps up to them begin at the level of your face. As the engine comes to a halt it heaves a great sigh of compressed air, prompting a Negro dressed in white linen to alight and place on the platform a yellow stool with a rubber-covered seat. Darkness has fallen and in this dormitory on wheels, people are dozing behind rows and rows of green curtains. And so here I am, reunited with my dear American railroad and once more reduced to undressing in a crouched position either on my back or tummy and to negotiating the naked feet protruding into the passage, asking to be trampled upon. If you want to smoke you must hide in the toilets. At the washbasin in the morning you wash blind, feeling your way through air darkened by cigar smoke. Everybody wants to know where you're bound, as the loud trumpeting of local speech drowns out even the booming of the locomotive's bell. Huge notices warn against playing bridge with partners whom you don't know: 'Beware of card sharks!' An appetizing aroma of maple syrup is already filling the outer corridor, which is as securely watertight as the vault of a bank. Through windows that are shuddering in their metal casing, the landscapes I see are completely different to those featured on postcards. The earth must have moved while we slept, for now the sky is full of mountains split open by volcanic fault-lines. And as the train starts its slow descent towards the Pacific, I begin to turn my back on Mexico.

From the point of view of the United States, Mexico is both an enchantment and an irritation. It moves capitalists to despair and novelists and scriptwriters to delight. It's a land whose flag appears to depict an American eagle swallowing grass-snakes. It's the world capital of Latino chaos and local colour and the last refuge of swashbuckling adventure and the poetry of the past. It's a magical treasure trove for collectors of antiques, a wonderful warehouse of cinema props. Mexico is a great and noble land, bursting with a future of its very own and, in terms of taste and thought, it's a rich source of fresh inspiration for the U.S.A.. And so in Florida and in California, along the beautiful golden beaches where the value of land increases tenfold year on year, all the houses are covered in 'Spanish plaster' and furnished in 'mission style'. The villas present themselves as 'Mexican villages,' the hostels are called *hogares* and the night clubs are called *patios*. In other words, the victor has, as always – inexorably even – submitted to the civilization of the vanquished.

THE APACHE TRAIL

This track is just one long procession of rocks connecting the desert plateau to the rich low plains of California. It takes me a whole day to travel it by car. Once the Redskins made their appearance in the books of Gustave Aymard[228], it was clear that they weren't going to go away. These days, however, they save their feather headwear for black-tie events, much as the Highlanders reserve their kilts for ceremonial occasions. It was in Colorado that we met our first Indian chiefs – 'Little Buffalo', 'Straight Bear'... And it was there too that a number of lordly Navajo elders regaled me with tales of their travels all over the world on ethnographic missions:

'Where do we Navajo hail from? Malaysia? Egypt? The puzzle has yet to be solved. But how on earth can the term "savages" be applied to a people endowed with the artistry, the history and the past to which we can lay claim?'

Putting away their feather headdresses, the Navajo line up in single file and perform three dances for me. The first, the dance of nature, begins and ends suddenly, like Stravinsky's music. It involves

---

228 Born Olivier Aymard (Aimard) in Paris in 1818 (died 1883), this prolific writer authored mainly novels that are set in the West of the United States of America (Arkansas, Missouri, etc:).

thumping out just one step in double time and is accompanied by a long, primitive, droning cry: Aya, Aya, Aya. The second piece is a love-song; it's sung by four boys in unison and is strangely reminiscent of Chinese music. The last one, a war dance, is all about the victorious return of the warrior chiefs. Holding scalps in their outstretched arms, stamping and hopping on one foot, the performers have been worked up into a frenzy by their dancing master and are chanting a wild and spirited ballad. It could have been Stravinsky's ballet, *The Wedding*. Indeed one of my friends, also a Frenchman, who knows a lot about Mexican Indians and has transcribed most of their folk music, told me that the first time he heard this piece, it reminded him of Stravinsky's *Rite of Spring*.

The demise of the Apaches hasn't altered the landscape in the slightest. On a scale far too grand for mere men, the backdrop is formed by porphyritic mountains in red or grey granite and by arid slopes covered in stand-alone cacti five metres tall like monstrous hairy asparagus stalks. This landscape has the desolate, brand-new grandeur of those New World canyons where the rains and the waterfalls have carved out huge craters and ravines in the rock. From a distance they look like ruined cities, boasting the fortresses, collapsed bastions and of course the gaping caves in which Quaternary Man subsisted until the last century. Daggers of snow spike the sky, reminding me of the poet Mallarmé[229], who couldn't resist making glacier rhyme with rapier. Vertiginous ascents bring us up to the zenith as cars, wheeling around above the void, turn into airplanes. We are climbing right up to the very same summits from which the Indians communed with one another across one hundred kilometres by lighting fires in the dark of the night, like spirits flying high above the limits of the human. From this vantage point the grey-blue surface of Lake Roosevelt is visible. It's the largest artificial reservoir in the world, feeding the valleys of

---

229 Stéphane Mallarmé's distinctively cerebral work often involved images of ice, blankness and whiteness.

Arizona and slaking the thirst of the mountain lions.

In Phoenix, Arizona, the mountains shrink and the desert begins again. One is reduced to despair by bizarre towns made of cement and corrugated iron, nightmarish historical caricatures boasting names like Elsinore, Luxor, Angora or Hamlet. Yet the morning after, they look more human. We've reached Pomona now, so the Pacific can't be far away. Indeed, its presence can be sensed in the mild air and tepid breeze. This is a place of pale orange groves, mandarin trees with coral-coloured fruit and mass-produced grapefruit. The long lemon-tinted trains of the Pacific Fruit Express are being loaded up in the railway stations. There are palm trees too and the smell of burning eucalyptus wood. The air stinks of petrol fumes for, at the foot of each orange tree, as far as the eye can see, there sits a petrol-burning stove meant to stave off the morning frost.

I'm entering now a place once known as Our Lady of the Angels. In the reign of Ferdinand VII[230] it counted some four thousand inhabitants and today it's called Los Angeles. After an absence of two years, I've returned at last to the Pacific fringe. In the North, this great ghostly ocean rears up convulsively, foaming at the mouth, but here in the South it lies in repose – softly supine, mythical and bedecked in flowers.

---

230 See above p. 154, note 184.